PYTHON FOR ARTIFICIAL INTELLIGENCE

Python for Artificial Intelligence

A COMPREHENSIVE GUIDE

Dr. Hesham Mohamed Elsherif

ELDONUSA Publishing

Contents

ABOUT THE AUTHOR

Python
for
Artificial Intelligence
A Comprehensive Guide
By
Dr. Hesham Mohamed Elsherif

Dr. Hesham Mohamed Elsherif stands at the forefront of library management and research, boasting an impressive 22-year tenure in the field. Holding dual doctoral degrees, one in Management and Organizational Leadership and the other in Information Systems and Technology, Dr. Elsherif brings a unique blend of knowledge to any intellectual endeavor.

An expert in Empirical research methodology, Dr. Elsherif specializes particularly in the Qualitative approach and Action research. This specialization has not only strengthened his research endeavors but has also allowed him to contribute invaluable insights and advancements in these areas.

Over the years, Dr. Elsherif has made significant contributions to the academic world not only as a professional researcher but also as an Adjunct Professor. This multifaceted role in the educational landscape has further solidified his reputation as a thought leader and pioneer.

Furthermore, Dr. Elsherif's expertise isn't confined to one region. He has served as a consultant to numerous educational institutions on an international scale, sharing best practices, innovative strategies, and his deep insights into the ever-evolving realms of management and technology.

Combining a passion for education with an unparalleled depth of knowledge, Dr. Elsherif continues to inspire, educate, and lead in both the library and academic communities.

PREFACE

Welcome to "Python for Artificial Intelligence: A Comprehensive Guide." In today's rapidly evolving technological landscape, Artificial Intelligence (AI) stands at the forefront of innovation, driving transformative changes across industries and domains. At the heart of AI lies Python, a versatile and powerful programming language renowned for its simplicity, flexibility, and rich ecosystem of libraries and frameworks.

This book is crafted as a comprehensive guide to mastering Python for AI, catering to learners of all levels, from aspiring beginners to seasoned practitioners. Whether you're a student, a professional developer, or an AI enthusiast eager to delve into the world of machine learning and deep learning, this book is your roadmap to success.

Why Python for AI?

Python has emerged as the language of choice for AI and machine learning due to several compelling reasons:

Ease of Learning: Python's clean syntax and readability make it accessible to beginners, allowing them to quickly grasp fundamental concepts and start building AI applications.

Vast Ecosystem: Python boasts a vast ecosystem of libraries and frameworks tailored for AI, including TensorFlow, Keras, PyTorch, scikit-learn, and more. These libraries provide powerful tools and algorithms for building sophisticated AI models with ease.

Community Support: Python's vibrant and active community of developers, researchers, and enthusiasts contributes to its rapid growth and evolution. With abundant resources, forums, and tutorials available online, learners have ample support to navigate the intricacies of AI development.

Industry Adoption: Python's popularity extends beyond academia, with major tech companies and startups alike embracing it for AI development. From data analysis and natural language processing to computer vision and reinforcement learning, Python powers a wide range of AI applications across diverse industries.

What This Book Offers:

This book is designed as a comprehensive resource to empower you with the knowledge, skills, and practical insights needed to excel in Python for AI. Here's what you can expect to find within its pages:

Foundational Concepts: A thorough introduction to Python programming, covering basic syntax, data types, control flow, and functions, tailored for AI development.

AI Libraries: In-depth exploration of popular AI libraries and frameworks in Python, including TensorFlow, Keras, PyTorch, and scikit-learn, with hands-on examples and tutorials.

Deep Learning: A detailed guide to building and training neural networks for deep learning tasks, such as image classification, natural language processing, and reinforcement learning.

Real-World Applications: Practical case studies and projects demonstrating the application of Python for AI in real-world scenarios, from sentiment analysis and chatbots to autonomous agents and computer vision applications.

How to Use This Book:

Whether you're reading cover to cover or jumping to specific chapters based on your interests and learning objectives, this book is designed to be your companion on the journey to mastering Python for AI. Each chapter builds upon the previous one, providing a structured and progressive learning experience. Hands-on exercises, code examples, and projects are included to reinforce learning and encourage experimentation.

Acknowledgments:

Creating a comprehensive guidebook of this magnitude would not have been possible without the contributions and support of many individuals. We extend our heartfelt gratitude to all the authors, editors, reviewers, and contributors who have played a role in bringing this book to fruition.

As you embark on your journey through the pages of "Python for Artificial Intelligence: A Comprehensive Guide," we invite you to embrace curiosity, embrace challenges, and embrace the transformative power of Python in shaping the future of AI. Whether you're driven by curiosity, ambition, or a desire to make a positive impact in the world, Python for AI offers boundless opportunities for exploration, discovery, and innovation.

Thank you for choosing "Python for Artificial Intelligence: A Comprehensive Guide." We hope that it serves as a valuable resource and companion on your path to mastery in Python and AI.

WHO SHOULD READ THIS BOOK?

"Python for Artificial Intelligence: A Comprehensive Guide" is tailored to meet the diverse needs of learners and professionals seeking to harness the power of Python for AI development. Whether you're a beginner exploring the world of artificial intelligence or an experienced practitioner looking to deepen your understanding and expand your skill set, this book offers valuable insights, practical techniques, and hands-on guidance to propel you forward on your journey. Here's a comprehensive overview of who can benefit from reading this book:

Students and Aspiring Data Scientists: If you're a student pursuing a degree in computer science, data science, or a related field, this book serves as an essential companion to your academic journey. It provides a solid foundation in Python programming and AI concepts, equipping you with the knowledge and skills needed to excel in your coursework and beyond.

Professionals Transitioning to AI: For professionals seeking to transition into the field of artificial intelligence, this book offers a structured learning path and practical insights to facilitate your career transition. Whether you're coming from a software development, data analysis, or engineering background, this book provides the necessary guidance to navigate the complexities of AI development with Python.

AI Enthusiasts and Hobbyists: If you're passionate about artificial intelligence and eager to explore its applications in Python, this book is for you. Whether you're tinkering with AI projects in your spare time or attending hackathons and competitions, this book serves as a valuable resource to deepen your understanding and expand your repertoire of AI skills and techniques.

Professionals in AI and Machine Learning: Professionals already working in the field of AI and machine learning will find this book to be a valuable reference and guide. Whether you're a data scientist, machine learning engineer, or AI researcher, this book offers insights into best practices, advanced techniques, and emerging trends in Python for AI development.

Educators and Trainers: Educators teaching courses or workshops on Python programming and artificial intelligence will find this book to be a valuable resource for structuring their curriculum and providing comprehensive coverage of key concepts and techniques. With its clear explanations, practical examples, and hands-on exercises, this book is suitable for both classroom instruction and self-paced learning.

Technology Enthusiasts and Lifelong Learners: Whether you're a technology enthusiast eager to explore the cutting-edge advancements in artificial intelligence or a lifelong learner with a thirst for knowledge, this book offers a wealth of information and insights to satisfy your curiosity and expand your horizons.

In summary, "Python for Artificial Intelligence: A Comprehensive Guide" is designed to cater to a diverse audience, including students, professionals, enthusiasts, educators, and lifelong learners. Whether you're embarking on a new career path, enhancing your existing skills, or simply exploring the fascinating world of artificial intelligence, this book provides the knowledge, guidance, and inspiration you need to succeed in Python for AI development.

WHY THIS BOOK IS ESSENTIAL READING?

"Python for Artificial Intelligence: A Comprehensive Guide" stands out as an essential resource in the realm of AI and Python programming for several compelling reasons:

1. **Holistic Coverage:** This book offers a comprehensive exploration of Python programming tailored specifically for artificial intelligence. It covers fundamental Python concepts, AI libraries, deep learning techniques, natural language processing, reinforcement learning, and real-world applications, providing readers with a well-rounded understanding of Python's role in AI development.

2. **Practical Approach:** With a hands-on and practical approach, this book bridges the gap between theory and practice. Through numerous examples, code snippets, and projects, readers gain practical experience in applying Python to solve real-world AI problems. This practical orientation fosters deeper understanding and enhances the reader's ability to translate concepts into actionable solutions.

3. **Accessible Language:** Written in clear, concise, and accessible language, this book is suitable for readers of all levels, from beginners to advanced practitioners. Complex concepts are

explained in a manner that is easy to understand, making it an ideal resource for self-paced learning and classroom instruction.

4. **Alignment with Industry Trends:** Python has emerged as the language of choice for AI development, and this book reflects the current industry trends and best practices in Python programming for AI. By covering popular AI libraries such as TensorFlow, Keras, PyTorch, and scikit-learn, this book equips readers with the skills and knowledge needed to stay relevant in today's rapidly evolving AI landscape.

5. **Empowerment for Career Advancement:** For students, professionals, and aspiring AI practitioners, this book serves as a pathway to career advancement and success. By mastering Python for AI, readers enhance their employability, open doors to exciting job opportunities, and position themselves as valuable assets in the competitive job market.

6. **Flexibility for Diverse Audiences:** Whether you're a student, professional, educator, or technology enthusiast, this book caters to a diverse audience with varying backgrounds and objectives. It serves as a valuable resource for learners seeking to acquire new skills, educators designing curriculum, and professionals looking to deepen their expertise in Python for AI development.

7. **Foundation for Lifelong Learning:** Beyond immediate career goals, this book lays the foundation for lifelong learning and continuous growth in the field of AI. With its clear explanations, practical examples, and hands-on exercises, readers are empowered to embark on a journey of exploration, experimentation, and innovation in Python for AI development.

In summary, "Python for Artificial Intelligence: A Comprehensive Guide" is an essential reading for anyone interested in mastering Python programming for AI. With its holistic coverage, practical approach, accessibility, alignment with industry trends, empowerment for career advancement, flexibility for diverse audiences, and foundation for lifelong learning, this book serves as a definitive guide to Python for AI development in today's digital age.

Chapter 1: Introduction to Python for AI

Python has become the language of choice for Artificial Intelligence (AI) development due to its simplicity, versatility, and rich ecosystem of libraries and frameworks. In this comprehensive part, we'll delve into the significance of Python in AI, its core features, and how it serves as an ideal language for building intelligent systems.

Significance of Python in AI:

Python's popularity in the field of AI stems from several key factors:

Simplicity:

Python's clean and intuitive syntax makes it easy to learn and understand, even for beginners. Its readability and expressiveness facilitate rapid development and experimentation, which is crucial in the dynamic and fast-paced field of AI.

Easy to Learn and Use

Python's syntax is clear, intuitive, and almost English-like, which significantly lowers the barrier to entry for beginners. This ease of learning and use accelerates the development process, enabling both seasoned programmers and newcomers to focus more on solving AI problems rather than grappling with complex syntax. The simplicity of Python makes it accessible to a broader audience, including those with non-computational backgrounds, thus democratizing AI development.

Versatile Libraries and Frameworks

The Python ecosystem boasts a rich collection of libraries and frameworks specifically designed for AI and machine learning (ML), such as TensorFlow, PyTorch, Keras, and scikit-learn. These libraries abstract away much of the complex mathematics and algorithms involved in AI development, providing simple interfaces for implementing sophisticated models. Python's simplicity ensures that these powerful tools are easily accessible, allowing developers to prototype, test, and deploy AI models with minimal overhead.

Community and Collaboration

Python's simplicity fosters a large and active community that contributes to its plethora of AI and ML libraries. This vibrant ecosystem facilitates collaboration, with abundant resources, tutorials, and forums available for troubleshooting and learning. For AI practitioners, this means easy access to the latest research, tools, and best practices, enabling them to stay at the forefront of innovation.

Interdisciplinary Integration

The field of AI intersects with various disciplines, including mathematics, statistics, cognitive science, and even philosophy. Python's simplicity acts as a bridge, enabling experts from these diverse fields to contribute their unique perspectives and expertise to AI projects. This interdisciplinary integration is crucial for tackling complex problems where insights from multiple domains are required.

Rapid Prototyping and Experimentation

AI development often involves iterative experimentation and prototyping. Python's simple and readable syntax, combined with its comprehensive libraries, enables rapid development cycles. Researchers can quickly test hypotheses, tweak models, and visualize results, thereby accelerating the iterative process of innovation. This agility is vital in a field that evolves as rapidly as AI.

The significance of Python's simplicity in AI cannot be overstated. It not only makes AI more approachable and less intimidating for beginners but also enhances productivity and fosters innovation among experienced practitioners. By lowering barriers to entry and facilitating rapid development and interdisciplinary collaboration, Python's simplicity has been a driving force behind the explosive growth of AI and will continue to be a cornerstone of AI development in the foreseeable future.

Versatility:

Python's versatility allows developers to tackle a wide range of AI tasks, from data preprocessing and model training to deployment and production. Whether you're working on machine learning, deep learning, natural language processing, or reinforcement learning, Python offers libraries and tools to support your endeavors.

Wide Range of Libraries and Frameworks

Python's ecosystem is replete with a diverse array of libraries and frameworks that cater to virtually every aspect of AI and machine learning (ML). Whether it's TensorFlow for deep learning, Pandas for data manipulation, or OpenCV for computer vision, Python offers specialized tools for different AI tasks. This breadth of resources allows developers to approach a wide array of AI problems without having to switch languages or learn new syntaxes, fostering a seamless development experience across various AI subfields.

Cross-Domain Application

The versatility of Python extends to its applicability across numerous domains. In healthcare, Python is used for predicting diseases and personalizing treatment plans. In finance, it aids in fraud detection and algorithmic trading. Python's applications in AI also stretch to robotics, autonomous vehicles, and natural language processing, demonstrating its adaptability to the evolving needs and challenges of different industries.

Platform Independence

Python's platform-independent nature further amplifies its versatility. It can run on Windows, macOS, Linux, and even niche operating systems. This cross-platform compatibility ensures that Python-based AI solutions can be developed and deployed across various environments without significant modifications, making Python an ideal choice for projects that require flexibility in deployment.

Integration Capabilities

Python excels in its ability to integrate with other languages and technologies. It can interface with C/C++ for performance-critical tasks, and with Java in web environments, among others. This interoperability allows AI developers to leverage the strengths of other languages and tools where needed, combining Python's ease of use with the performance or functionality specific to other ecosystems.

Support for Research and Development

Python's versatility is not only limited to practical applications but also extends to academic and research-oriented activities. It is widely used in scientific computing, data analysis, and statistical modeling, which are foundational to AI research. Python's support for visualization tools like Matplotlib and Seaborn enables researchers to present their findings effectively, while IPython and Jupyter Notebooks offer interactive computing environments that are invaluable for exploratory analysis.

Scalability and Performance

Though Python is sometimes critiqued for its performance limitations compared to compiled languages, its versatility shines through its ecosystem's solutions for scalability and performance optimization. Libraries like NumPy and Cython allow for efficient numerical computations and the ability to write Python code that compiles to C, respectively. Moreover, Python's compatibility with distributed computing frameworks like Apache Spark enables scaling of AI models to process large datasets efficiently.

Python's versatility makes it a powerhouse in the AI field. Its comprehensive libraries and frameworks, cross-domain applications, platform independence, integration capabilities, and robust support for research and development make it the go-to language for AI professionals and enthusiasts alike. This versatility not only facilitates a wide range of AI applications but also ensures Python's continued relevance as AI technologies evolve and expand into new areas. Python's role in AI is a testament to how a language's versatility can drive innovation and progress in one of the most dynamic fields of the 21st century.

Rich Ecosystem:

Python boasts a vast ecosystem of AI libraries, frameworks, and tools that streamline the development process. From TensorFlow and Keras for deep learning to scikit-learn and PyTorch for machine learning, Python provides access to cutting-edge technologies and algorithms, enabling developers to build powerful and sophisticated AI systems.

Extensive Libraries and Frameworks

At the heart of Python's ecosystem for AI are its libraries and frameworks, which provide pre-built functionalities for a wide range of AI tasks, including machine learning, deep learning, natural language processing, computer vision, and data analysis. Libraries such as TensorFlow, PyTorch, Keras, and scikit-learn offer sophisticated algorithms and models that are accessible with minimal coding, significantly reducing development time. These tools are not only powerful but are also regularly updated to incorporate the latest advancements in AI, ensuring that Python developers have access to cutting-edge technologies.

Active Developer Community

Python's ecosystem is further enriched by its vibrant and active community. This community plays a crucial role in the ongoing development and maintenance of Python libraries and frameworks, contributing to a self-sustaining cycle of innovation and improvement. The Python community is known for its inclusivity and support, offering extensive documentation, forums, tutorials, and courses that lower the barrier to entry for newcomers and provide valuable resources for experienced developers. This collaborative environment fosters learning and innovation, making it easier for developers to solve complex problems and share their solutions.

Integration and Compatibility

Python's ecosystem excels in its ability to integrate with other systems and software, offering compatibility across a broad range of applications and platforms. Python interfaces seamlessly with databases, web services, and even languages like C/C++ for performance-critical tasks. This level of integration capability allows AI applications developed in Python to be easily deployed in varied environments, from desktop applications to cloud-based services, enhancing the practicality and reach of Python-based AI solutions.

Tools for Development and Research

Python is equipped with an assortment of development and research tools that streamline the AI development process. Integrated Development Environments (IDEs) like PyCharm and Jupyter Notebooks provide powerful platforms for coding, testing, and debugging. Moreover, tools such as Matplotlib, Seaborn, and Plotly facilitate data visualization, enabling researchers and developers to analyze and present data effectively. For scientific computing and numerical analysis, libraries like NumPy and SciPy are indispensable, offering a robust foundation for AI research.

Scalability and Performance Optimization

Python's ecosystem addresses the language's performance limitations through libraries and tools that optimize computation and enable scalability. Libraries like NumPy offer efficient operations for large-scale numerical data, while Cython allows Python code to be compiled into C, improving execution speed. For distributed computing and handling big data, frameworks such as Apache Spark and Dask are available within Python's ecosystem, enabling the scaling of AI models to process vast datasets effectively.

Open Source Nature

The open-source nature of Python's ecosystem is a significant advantage, allowing for free access to a wealth of tools and libraries. This openness encourages experimentation and innovation, as developers can modify and improve existing code to suit their specific needs. The collaborative spirit fostered by open source development is instrumental in the rapid advancement of AI technologies, with contributions from individuals and organizations worldwide.

Python's rich ecosystem is a cornerstone of its significance in AI, providing an unparalleled combination of tools, libraries, community support, and integration capabilities. This ecosystem not only facilitates the development of sophisticated AI applications but also fosters a culture of collaboration and innovation. As AI continues to evolve, Python's ecosystem is well-positioned to adapt and grow, further cementing Python's role as an essential tool for AI practitioners.

Community Support:

Python's vibrant and active community of developers, researchers, and enthusiasts contributes to its continuous growth and evolution. With a wealth of resources, forums, tutorials, and open-source projects available online, Python developers have access to invaluable support and collaboration opportunities, fostering innovation and knowledge sharing in the AI community.

Global Developer Network

Python benefits from a vast and diverse global community of developers, researchers, and enthusiasts who actively contribute to its growth. This network spans academia and industry, fostering an environment where innovations and best practices are rapidly disseminated. The community's contributions range from developing and maintaining libraries and frameworks to fixing bugs and improving documentation. This collective effort ensures that Python's tools for AI remain robust, up-to-date, and accessible to a broad audience.

Extensive Learning Resources

One of the hallmarks of Python's community is the wealth of learning resources it offers. These include comprehensive documentation, detailed tutorials, online courses, webinars, and forums. Such resources make Python more accessible to beginners and provide pathways for continuous learning, allowing developers to stay abreast of the latest AI technologies and methodologies. Whether one is just starting out in AI or is an experienced practitioner looking to expand their skill set, the Python community provides an abundance of materials to facilitate growth and expertise.

Open Source Collaboration

The open-source nature of Python and its libraries encourages a culture of collaboration and sharing. Developers from around the world contribute code, participate in code reviews, and engage in discussions about future directions. This collaborative model not only accelerates the development of Python's AI ecosystem but also ensures its quality and reliability. Through platforms like GitHub, developers can contribute to projects, regardless of their geographical location, amplifying Python's capabilities and its utility in AI.

Forums and Discussion Groups

Python's community thrives in online forums and discussion groups, such as Stack Overflow, Reddit, and specialized mailing lists. These platforms serve as hubs for knowledge exchange, problem-solving, and innovation. Developers can seek advice, share insights, and discuss the latest AI trends and challenges. The supportive atmosphere of these forums fosters a sense of belonging and encourages continuous engagement with Python's AI ecosystem.

Conferences and Meetups

Python's community support is further evidenced by its vibrant ecosystem of conferences, meetups, and hackathons. Events like PyCon, SciPy, and various local meetups bring together Python enthusiasts to share knowledge, showcase projects, and network. These gatherings are crucial for community building and provide invaluable opportunities for learning and collaboration. They also serve as platforms for presenting cutting-edge research and applications in AI, facilitating the exchange of ideas and fostering innovation.

Support for Research and Education

The Python community places a strong emphasis on supporting research and education in AI. Many universities and research institutions adopt Python in their curricula and research projects, benefiting from the community's contributions in the form of libraries, tools, and datasets. The community's commitment to open source and knowledge sharing aligns with academic values, making Python a preferred choice for educational purposes and research endeavors in AI.

Community support is a cornerstone of Python's success in AI, reflecting a collective effort to advance the field through open collaboration, knowledge sharing, and continuous innovation. This support not only makes Python more accessible and powerful but also fosters a culture of inclusivity and growth. As AI continues to evolve, the strength and vibrancy of Python's community are likely to further cement its position as a leading language in AI development and research.

Core Features of Python for AI:

Python offers several features that make it particularly well-suited for AI development:

Dynamic Typing:

Python's dynamic typing allows for flexible and concise code, enabling developers to focus on solving AI problems without getting bogged down by low-level details. Variables are dynamically typed, meaning they can hold values of any data type, making code more adaptable and easier to maintain.

Flexibility in Coding

Dynamic typing offers a high level of coding flexibility, which is particularly advantageous in AI development, where exploration and iterative experimentation are common. Developers can write more generic and flexible code without the need to declare variable types explicitly. This flexibility speeds up the development process, as programmers can focus on implementing algorithms and data processing without worrying about strict type constraints. This aspect of Python makes it an excellent language for prototyping AI models and algorithms, where rapid iteration and testing are crucial.

Ease of Use and Readability

Python's dynamic typing contributes to its overall ease of use and readability. Code written in Python is closer to natural language, making it more accessible to beginners and interdisciplinary professionals who may not have a formal background in computer science. In the context of AI, where domain experts (such as data scientists, statisticians, and domain-specific researchers) often collaborate, Python's readability and ease of use facilitate better understanding and communication among team members, enhancing collaborative AI project development.

Reduced Development Time

The absence of a strict type system means that developers can write less code to achieve the same outcomes compared to statically typed languages. This reduction in boilerplate code not only speeds up the development process but also reduces the cognitive load on developers, allowing them to concentrate on solving AI problems. In an AI project, where time-to-market can be critical, the ability to prototype and iterate quickly without being bogged down by type-related issues is invaluable.

Enhanced Productivity

Dynamic typing inherently supports higher-level abstractions and simplifies the manipulation of data structures, which are frequent operations in AI applications. Python's dynamic nature allows developers to use data structures more intuitively, fostering productivity. For instance, working with complex nested data returned from APIs or manipulating large datasets for machine learning can be more straightforward, as the intricacies of data types and conversions are handled dynamically by Python.

Seamless Integration with AI Libraries

Many AI and machine learning libraries in Python, such as Tensor-Flow, PyTorch, and Pandas, leverage dynamic typing to provide a user-friendly interface. These libraries abstract away the complexities of underlying algorithms and data structures, presenting a simple and dynamic interface to users. This seamless integration is possible because of Python's dynamic typing, which allows for a high degree of flexibility and interactivity when working with these libraries, making the development of AI applications more intuitive and efficient.

Adaptability to AI Evolution

The field of AI is characterized by rapid evolution and innovation. Dynamic typing in Python ensures that the language remains adaptable to new developments in AI. As new algorithms, data types, and AI paradigms emerge, Python's dynamic nature allows it to incorporate these advancements without the need for extensive modifications or updates to the language itself. This adaptability is crucial for maintaining Python's relevance and utility in the ever-evolving landscape of AI technologies.

Dynamic typing is a core feature of Python that plays a significant role in its adoption and success in the AI domain. It offers flexibility, ease of use, and reduced development time, which are essential for the fast-paced and exploratory nature of AI development. Furthermore, dynamic typing enhances productivity and ensures Python's adaptability to the continuous innovations in AI. By providing a developer-friendly environment that supports rapid iteration and interdisciplinary collaboration, dynamic typing in Python solidifies its position as a preferred language for AI research and application development.

High-level Data Structures:

Python provides high-level data structures such as lists, dictionaries, sets, and tuples, which simplify data manipulation and analysis. These built-in data structures are essential for handling large datasets, performing complex computations, and implementing AI algorithms effectively.

Simplified Data Management

Python's high-level data structures simplify the management of complex data, a common requirement in AI applications. For example, lists and dictionaries in Python allow for the dynamic and efficient storage of data, with easy access and modification operations. This simplicity is invaluable in AI development, where manipulating large datasets and parameters is frequent. Developers can focus on implementing algorithms without getting bogged down by the intricacies of data management.

Enhanced Readability and Maintainability

The intuitive nature of Python's data structures enhances code readability and maintainability. This is particularly important in AI projects, which can be complex and involve multidisciplinary teams. Code that is easy to read and understand facilitates collaboration among team members who may have varying levels of programming expertise. For instance, dictionaries in Python can represent data in a key-value pair, mirroring real-world data relationships, making the code more accessible and understandable.

Efficient Data Manipulation

Python's data structures are designed for efficient data manipulation, supporting operations like iteration, selection, and filtering with ease. Such operations are central to data preprocessing, feature selection, and exploratory data analysis in AI. The ability to perform these operations efficiently and with minimal code contributes to Python's appeal for AI development, where data manipulation is a routine task.

Support for Heterogeneous Data

AI applications often involve dealing with heterogeneous data types — numeric values, text, images, and more. Python's high-level data structures naturally support heterogeneous data, allowing for the combination of different data types in a single structure. This flexibility is crucial for developing AI models that process and analyze diverse datasets, making Python an adaptable tool for a wide range of AI tasks.

Scalability and Performance

While Python's high-level data structures are designed for ease of use and flexibility, they also provide a foundation for scalability and performance optimizations. Libraries like NumPy and Pandas build upon Python's native data structures to offer more efficient storage and manipulation of large datasets. These libraries are essential in AI for handling high-volume data processing and analysis, offering performance optimizations while retaining the simplicity and flexibility of Python's native data structures.

Facilitating Data Science and Machine Learning

The seamless integration of Python's data structures with data science and machine learning libraries underscores their significance in AI. For instance, Pandas DataFrames build on dictionaries and lists to provide a powerful and flexible data structure tailored for data analysis and manipulation. This integration facilitates the development of sophisticated AI models, as developers can leverage high-level data structures to interact with complex algorithms and statistical methods efficiently.

Python's high-level data structures are a foundational feature that contributes significantly to its suitability for AI development. They offer a blend of simplicity, flexibility, and power that is ideally suited to the demands of AI programming, from data manipulation and analysis to model building and evaluation. By providing an intuitive and efficient means of working with complex data, these data structures not only enhance productivity but also foster innovation in AI, making Python an indispensable tool for AI researchers and developers.

Interpreted Language:

Python is an interpreted language, which means that code execution happens line by line, making it ideal for interactive development and rapid prototyping. This interactive nature allows developers to experiment with algorithms, visualize results, and iterate quickly, speeding up the AI development cycle.

Immediate Feedback and Rapid Prototyping

One of the most significant advantages of Python being an interpreted language is the ability to receive immediate feedback when writing and executing code. This feature is invaluable in AI development, where experimentation and iterative testing are commonplace. Developers can quickly write a piece of code and execute it to see the results or debug errors, facilitating rapid prototyping of AI models. This immediacy encourages exploration and experimentation, which are essential in the innovative and fast-paced field of AI.

Ease of Debugging

The interpreted nature of Python simplifies the debugging process. Since code is executed line by line, it's easier to identify and correct errors as they occur. This granularity in execution allows developers to isolate problematic sections of code more efficiently than in compiled languages, where errors may only become apparent after the entire program is compiled. For AI development, where algorithms can get complex and data dependencies are intricate, the ability to debug effectively is crucial for ensuring the accuracy and reliability of AI models.

Flexibility in Development

Python's interpreted nature offers a high degree of development flexibility, accommodating changes and modifications with ease. In the context of AI, where models and algorithms often undergo iterative refinement, this flexibility means that developers can modify and test different approaches without the overhead of recompiling code. This adaptability supports a more dynamic and creative development process, enabling AI practitioners to refine their models and algorithms continuously until the desired performance is achieved.

Cross-Platform Compatibility

Being an interpreted language, Python inherently supports cross-platform compatibility. Python code can run on any platform that has a Python interpreter, including Windows, macOS, Linux, and various Unix variants. This feature is particularly beneficial for AI projects that may need to be deployed across different operating systems and environments. The ability to write code once and run it anywhere (WORA) without modification saves time and resources, making Python an attractive option for developing portable AI applications.

Lower Barrier to Entry

The simplicity and readability of Python, compounded by its interpreted nature, significantly lower the barrier to entry for beginners and professionals from non-computational backgrounds. This accessibility is important in AI, a multidisciplinary field that benefits from the insights and expertise of domain experts across various sectors. Python enables these professionals to engage with AI development more directly, fostering a more inclusive and diverse AI research and development community.

Interactive Computing Environments

Python's compatibility with interactive computing environments, such as Jupyter Notebooks, is largely due to its interpreted nature. These environments support interactive coding sessions, where developers can write and execute code in segments, visualize data, and see results in real-time. This interactive approach is especially conducive to AI and data science workflows, allowing for exploratory data analysis, model training and evaluation, and visualization within a cohesive, document-like interface.

The interpreted nature of Python stands out as a core feature that significantly enhances its utility for AI development. It supports rapid prototyping, ease of debugging, development flexibility, cross-platform compatibility, and accessibility, all of which are critical attributes in the fast-evolving field of AI. Furthermore, it enables the use of interactive computing environments that streamline AI workflows. These advantages, collectively, contribute to Python's status as a leading programming language in AI research and application development, facilitating innovation and progress in the field.

Extensive Standard Library:

Python's extensive standard library offers a wide range of modules and functions for performing common tasks, such as file I/O, networking, and data processing. This rich set of built-in functionalities accelerates AI development by providing ready-made solutions to common challenges.

Wide Range of Functionality

The Python Standard Library covers a broad spectrum of programming needs, offering built-in modules for data structures, algorithms, file handling, system calls, and even Internet protocols like HTTP and FTP. For AI developers, this means access to a wealth of functionality out of the box. For instance, the **collections** module provides specialized container datatypes which are useful for maintaining large datasets, while the **math** and **statistics** modules offer essential mathematical functions and statistical operations that are foundational to AI algorithms.

Data Handling and Processing

Effective data handling and processing are critical in AI and ML projects. Python's standard library excels in this regard, offering powerful modules like **json** for JSON data interchange, **csv** for reading and writing CSV files, and **sqlite3** for interacting with SQLite databases. These modules facilitate the manipulation and storage of data, enabling developers to focus on higher-level algorithm development without worrying about the intricacies of data formats and storage mechanisms.

Network Programming Support

AI applications often require network programming capabilities, whether for consuming web services, handling remote data, or integrating with cloud-based AI services. Python's standard library includes modules like **urllib** for working with URLs and **socket** for low-level network communication. This built-in support for network programming allows for the easy integration of web data and services into AI models, expanding the possibilities for data sourcing and model deployment.

Concurrency and Parallelism

As AI algorithms become increasingly complex and data-intensive, the ability to execute tasks concurrently or in parallel becomes essential. Python's standard library addresses this need through modules such as **threading, concurrency.futures**, and **multiprocessing**. These modules enable AI developers to leverage multi-threading and multi-processing, improving the performance and efficiency of AI applications, especially when processing large datasets or performing computationally intensive tasks.

Development and Debugging Tools

The standard library includes several modules that support the development and debugging of AI applications. For instance, the **logging** module provides a flexible logging system, while **unittest** supports the development of test cases, ensuring that AI models and algorithms are robust and reliable. The **pdb** module, Python's debugger, offers essential debugging capabilities, helping developers identify and resolve issues more efficiently.

Extensibility and Interoperability

While the Python Standard Library provides a comprehensive set of tools and functionalities, it is also designed to be extensible. Developers can easily integrate third-party libraries and frameworks that are specific to AI and ML, such as NumPy for numerical computing, Pandas for data analysis, and TensorFlow or PyTorch for deep learning. This extensibility, coupled with the robust foundation provided by the standard library, ensures that Python remains adaptable to the evolving needs of AI development.

The extensive standard library is a cornerstone of Python's appeal for AI development, offering a rich set of functionalities that streamline the development process. By providing built-in solutions for a wide range of tasks, from data handling to network programming to concurrency, the standard library not only enhances productivity but also fosters innovation by allowing developers to focus on solving complex AI problems. This, combined with Python's other core features, solidifies its position as a leading language in the AI and ML domains, capable of meeting the diverse needs of modern AI projects.

Why Python is Ideal for AI:

Python's combination of simplicity, versatility, rich ecosystem, and community support makes it an ideal language for AI development:

Ease of Learning and Use:

Python's straightforward syntax and readability lower the barrier to entry for beginners, enabling aspiring AI developers to get started quickly and make meaningful contributions to the field.

Intuitive Syntax

Python's syntax is designed to be readable and straightforward, mirroring the natural language to a greater extent than many other programming languages. This design philosophy reduces the cognitive load on developers, allowing them to grasp Python's fundamentals quickly and to focus more on problem-solving rather than on deciphering complex syntax. For AI development, where the complexity of algorithms and data structures can be daunting, Python's clarity facilitates a smoother learning curve and faster development cycles.

Consistent and Readable Code

The Python language enforces an emphasis on consistency and readability, primarily through its use of indentation to define code blocks instead of braces or keywords. This approach not only makes Python code more readable but also ensures that it is organized in a way that is logical and consistent across different projects. In the context of AI, where projects often involve collaboration among multidisciplinary teams, the ability for code to be easily understood and maintained is invaluable.

Comprehensive Resources for Beginners

Python benefits from a vast ecosystem of learning resources, including extensive documentation, tutorials, online courses, and community forums. This wealth of materials makes it easier for newcomers to start their journey in programming and AI. Additionally, the active Python community is known for its willingness to support beginners, providing guidance and answering questions, which significantly lowers the barrier to entry for those new to AI.

Integration with AI and ML Libraries

The ease of use of Python extends to its integration with major AI and ML libraries, such as TensorFlow, PyTorch, and scikit-learn. These libraries are designed with Python's simplicity in mind, offering high-level interfaces that abstract away much of the underlying complexity. This allows developers to implement sophisticated AI algorithms and data processing pipelines with relatively simple and concise code, accelerating the development of AI applications.

Versatile Development Environments

Python supports a range of development environments that cater to different preferences and needs, from simple script editors to comprehensive Integrated Development Environments (IDEs) like Py-Charm and Jupyter Notebooks. Jupyter Notebooks, in particular, have become a staple in AI and data science projects for their interactive computing and visualization capabilities. These environments enhance Python's ease of use by providing tools for writing, testing, and debugging code more efficiently, along with visualizing data and results, which are crucial aspects of AI development.

Cross-Domain Application

Python's simplicity and versatility make it suitable not just for software development but also for tasks across various domains, including web development, data analysis, and scientific computing. This cross-domain applicability is particularly beneficial in AI, where solutions often require interdisciplinary knowledge and integration with other systems. Python's ease of use thus enables professionals from different fields to contribute to AI projects, fostering innovation and collaboration.

Python's ease of learning and use is a key reason why it is ideal for AI development. Its intuitive syntax, emphasis on readability, comprehensive learning resources, seamless integration with AI libraries, versatile development environments, and cross-domain application collectively lower the barriers to entry and enhance productivity in AI projects. These attributes not only make Python accessible to a wide audience but also ensure that it remains at the forefront of AI innovation, catering to both educational purposes and cutting-edge research.

Scalability and Performance:

Despite being an interpreted language, Python offers high performance and scalability, thanks to its efficient memory management and support for multi-threading and multiprocessing. With libraries like NumPy and TensorFlow, Python can handle large-scale AI workloads with ease.

Scalability Through High-Level Abstractions

Python provides high-level abstractions that simplify the development of scalable AI applications. Libraries such as NumPy for numerical computing and Pandas for data manipulation allow developers to work with large datasets efficiently, using operations that are internally optimized for performance. These abstractions let developers focus on algorithmic innovation rather than low-level optimization details, facilitating the design of scalable AI models that can process vast amounts of data.

Performance Optimization with Libraries

While Python itself may not offer the raw performance of compiled languages like C or C++, it compensates through the ability to integrate with performance-optimized libraries. Libraries such as TensorFlow and PyTorch leverage underlying C/C++ code for computationally intensive tasks, offering Python interfaces for ease of use. This hybrid approach allows AI applications to achieve high performance for numerical computations and model training while retaining Python's simplicity and flexibility.

Parallel and Distributed Computing

Python's ecosystem includes robust support for parallel and distributed computing, essential for scaling AI applications. The **multiprocessing** module facilitates parallel execution of code across multiple CPU cores, while libraries like Dask and Ray enable distributed computing across clusters of machines. For AI tasks that require processing large datasets or training complex models, these tools allow Python applications to scale horizontally, utilizing additional hardware to accelerate computation.

Integration with Cloud Services

The rise of cloud computing has significantly enhanced the scalability and performance of AI applications. Python's strong support for cloud services integration, through SDKs for platforms like AWS, Google Cloud, and Azure, enables developers to leverage cloud-based compute resources, storage, and AI services. This integration simplifies the deployment of scalable AI solutions that can access virtually unlimited computing resources on demand, aligning with the elastic nature of cloud environments.

Efficient Data Handling

Python's efficiency in handling data is another aspect that contributes to its scalability in AI projects. The language's native data structures, combined with specialized libraries like Pandas, provide flexible and efficient ways to store, manipulate, and analyze data. Efficient data handling is crucial for AI applications, where the ability to process and extract insights from large datasets directly impacts performance and scalability.

Community and Ecosystem

The vibrant Python community continually contributes tools, libraries, and best practices for scaling and optimizing AI applications. This wealth of resources and collective knowledge ensures that Python developers have access to cutting-edge solutions for performance optimization and scalability challenges. The community's focus on innovation and improvement supports the ongoing development of more scalable and performant Python-based AI systems.

Python's scalability and performance capabilities make it an ideal choice for AI development, from small-scale projects to enterprise-level applications. Through its high-level abstractions, integration with performance-optimized libraries, support for parallel and distributed computing, cloud integration, efficient data handling, and a supportive community, Python offers a compelling ecosystem for developing scalable and high-performance AI solutions. These features ensure that Python remains at the forefront of AI research and development, capable of meeting the demands of increasingly complex and data-intensive AI challenges.

Integration and Compatibility:

Python seamlessly integrates with other programming languages and platforms, allowing developers to leverage existing code, libraries, and tools in their AI projects. Whether it's interfacing with C/C++ libraries or deploying models on cloud platforms, Python offers unparalleled compatibility and interoperability.

Wide Support for Libraries and Frameworks

Python's compatibility with a broad spectrum of libraries and frameworks is one of its most compelling features for AI development. Libraries like TensorFlow, PyTorch, and scikit-learn, which are fundamental to AI and machine learning, offer Python interfaces, allowing for straightforward integration into Python projects. This extensive support extends beyond AI-specific libraries to include data visualization tools like Matplotlib and Seaborn, data manipulation libraries such as Pandas, and numerical computation libraries like NumPy. This wide-ranging library support empowers developers to build sophisticated AI models while leveraging Python's simplicity and readability.

Cross-Platform Functionality

Python is inherently cross-platform, meaning it can run on Windows, Linux, macOS, and other operating systems without modification. This cross-platform functionality ensures that Python-based AI applications can be developed and deployed across different environments, facilitating broader accessibility and usability. For businesses and developers, this means the ability to reach a wider audience and ensure consistent performance across various platforms, which is crucial for the deployment of AI solutions in diverse IT ecosystems.

Interoperability with Other Languages

Python excels in interoperability with other programming languages, enabling developers to use Python in conjunction with languages like C, C++, and Java. Tools like Cython allow Python code to be converted into C code, combining Python's ease of use with C's performance benefits. Similarly, Jython enables Python code to run on the Java platform. This interoperability is particularly valuable in AI projects that require high-performance computations or need to integrate with legacy systems written in other languages, allowing for the best of both worlds—Python's simplicity and the performance or functionality specific to other ecosystems.

Support for Cloud and API Integrations

The modern AI landscape increasingly relies on cloud computing and API services for data storage, processing, and model deployment.

Python's strong support for cloud services and RESTful API integration makes it well-suited for cloud-based AI applications. Python frameworks like Flask and Django simplify the creation of RESTful APIs, while SDKs and libraries for cloud platforms (AWS, Google Cloud Platform, Azure) facilitate the integration of cloud services. This ease of integration with cloud and API services allows for scalable, distributed AI systems that leverage the power of cloud computing.

Extensive Development Tools and IDEs

Python is supported by a wide range of development tools and Integrated Development Environments (IDEs), including PyCharm, Visual Studio Code, and Jupyter Notebooks. These tools provide functionalities like code completion, debugging, and version control integration, enhancing Python's ease of use. For AI development, Jupyter Notebooks are particularly valuable for their interactive computing and data visualization capabilities, enabling exploratory data analysis and iterative model development in a collaborative environment.

Robust Community and Documentation

The Python community plays a crucial role in the language's integration and compatibility strengths. A vibrant ecosystem of developers contributes to a wealth of documentation, forums, and third-party resources that assist in resolving integration challenges and compatibility issues. This community support ensures that Python developers have access to the latest best practices and solutions for integrating various technologies into their AI projects.

Python's integration capabilities and compatibility with a diverse range of platforms, tools, and libraries make it an outstanding choice for AI development. Its ability to seamlessly integrate with other languages, cloud platforms, and APIs, coupled with its cross-platform functionality and extensive library support, provides a flexible and powerful foundation for building and deploying AI applications. These features, combined with the support of a robust community, ensure that Python remains at the forefront of AI innovation, facilitating the development of cutting-edge AI solutions.

In summary, Python's simplicity, versatility, rich ecosystem, and community support make it the language of choice for AI development. From beginners exploring the basics of machine learning to seasoned practitioners building sophisticated deep learning models, Python provides the tools, libraries, and resources needed to turn AI ideas into reality. In the subsequent chapters of this book, we'll delve deeper into Python programming for AI, covering essential concepts, libraries, techniques, and real-world applications to equip you with the knowledge and skills needed to excel in the field of artificial intelligence.

Introduction To Python Programming Language:

Python is a high-level, interpreted programming language known for its simplicity, readability, and versatility. In this comprehensive part, we'll explore the fundamentals of Python programming language and how it serves as an ideal foundation for building artificial intelligence (AI) applications.

Simplicity and Readability:

One of Python's defining features is its simplicity and readability. Python's syntax is designed to be intuitive and easy to understand, making it accessible to beginners and experienced programmers alike. Its clean and concise syntax reduces the cognitive overhead associated with understanding and writing code, allowing developers to focus on solving problems rather than wrestling with syntax.

Simplicity in Design

Python's design philosophy, encapsulated by the aphorism "Simple is better than complex," prioritizes straightforward and uncluttered syntax. This simplicity is manifest in several aspects of the language:

Clear Syntax: Python uses English keywords frequently, reducing the barrier to entry for beginners and non-programmers. This choice makes Python an ideal language for introductory programming courses and self-taught coders.

Minimal Syntax Requirements: Unlike languages that rely heavily on punctuation, Python uses indentation to delineate blocks of code. This approach not only enforces cleaner code but also makes the structure of the program visually apparent, enhancing readability.

Interpreted Nature: As an interpreted language, Python allows for the execution of code as soon as it is written, facilitating a rapid iterative development process. This immediacy is particularly advantageous for learning programming concepts and for prototyping.

Emphasis on Readability

Readability is a cornerstone of Python's design, reflecting the belief that code is read more often than it is written. This focus on readability has several benefits:

Maintainability: Readable code is easier to debug, understand, and modify, which is essential in collaborative environments where multiple developers work on the same project. The emphasis on readability thus contributes to lower maintenance costs and a longer lifespan for Python projects.

Collaboration: The readability of Python code enhances collaboration among developers with varying levels of expertise. It allows more experienced developers to write code that is accessible to novices, fostering a more inclusive and productive development environment.

Cross-Domain Application: Python's readability makes it accessible to professionals beyond traditional software development, such as scientists, engineers, and analysts. This has propelled Python to the forefront of disciplines like data science and AI, where it is used not only for programming but also for communicating complex algorithms and data processing workflows.

Educational Tool

Python's simplicity and readability have made it a preferred language for education, introducing students and beginners to programming concepts without overwhelming them with complex syntax. Its use in education extends to teaching fundamental programming principles, data science, web development, and more, preparing learners for a wide range of career paths.

The Foundation for a Rich Ecosystem

The approachability of Python has contributed to the growth of a rich ecosystem of libraries and frameworks, further enhancing its versatility. Libraries like Django and Flask for web development, Pandas and NumPy for data analysis, and TensorFlow and PyTorch for machine learning are built on Python's foundation of simplicity and readability, offering powerful functionalities while remaining accessible to a broad audience.

Python's simplicity and readability are not just features of the language; they represent a philosophy that prioritizes developer experience and the practical aspects of programming. By focusing on these core principles, Python has become a language that supports a wide range of programming tasks while remaining accessible to people from diverse backgrounds and skill levels. This unique combination of simplicity, readability, and power is what makes Python an essential tool for beginners and experts alike, driving its adoption in education, development, and research across the globe.

Versatility and Flexibility:

Python's versatility and flexibility make it suitable for a wide range of programming tasks, including AI development. Whether you're working on data analysis, web development, scientific computing, or AI research, Python provides the tools and libraries needed to tackle diverse challenges. Its extensive standard library and rich ecosystem of third-party packages offer solutions for virtually any problem domain, empowering developers to build complex and sophisticated AI applications with ease.

Wide-Ranging Applications

Python's applications are as diverse as the problems it helps solve. Its versatility is evident in several key areas:

- **Web Development**: With frameworks like Django and Flask, Python offers robust solutions for building everything from simple web apps to complex, scalable web services.
- **Data Science and Analysis**: Libraries such as Pandas, NumPy, and Matplotlib have made Python indispensable for data manipulation, statistical analysis, and visualization.
- **Machine Learning and AI**: Python is at the forefront of AI research and application, thanks to libraries like TensorFlow, PyTorch, and scikit-learn that simplify complex algorithms and computational processes.
- **Scientific Computing**: In scientific fields, Python's versatility is showcased through libraries like SciPy for advanced computing and SymPy for symbolic mathematics.
- **Automation and Scripting**: Python's simplicity and readability make it ideal for writing scripts to automate mundane tasks, from data entry to network configuration.
- **Game Development**: Though not as widely used for game development as some other languages, Python still offers libraries like Pygame, providing a platform for developing simple games and multimedia applications.

Ease of Integration

Python's flexibility is further highlighted by its ease of integration with other programming languages and technologies:

- **C and C++ Integration**: Using tools like Cython, Python code can be converted into C code, and it's also possible to call C and C++ libraries directly from Python. This allows developers to optimize performance-critical sections of an application without leaving the Python environment.
- **Cross-Platform Operation**: Python programs can run on multiple operating systems without modification, thanks to its interpreted nature and the comprehensive standard library that

abstracts away many of the differences between OS environments.

- **Web Services Integration**: Python's standard library includes modules for accessing the web and processing internet protocols. Many third-party modules extend these capabilities, facilitating the integration of complex web services and APIs into Python applications.

Adaptable to Various Programming Paradigms

Python supports multiple programming paradigms, offering flexibility in how problems can be approached and solved:

- **Object-Oriented Programming (OOP)**: Python supports OOP with classes and objects, allowing for encapsulation, inheritance, and polymorphism, which are fundamental in designing reusable code and complex applications.
- **Functional Programming**: Python includes features like first-class functions, lambdas, and higher-order functions, making it suitable for functional programming for scenarios where this paradigm offers efficiencies.
- **Procedural Programming**: For developers and applications that benefit from a straightforward, top-down approach, Python supports procedural programming, making it accessible to those familiar with traditional programming concepts.

Rapid Prototyping

The flexibility of Python makes it an excellent choice for rapid prototyping. Developers can quickly test new ideas and concepts due to Python's concise syntax, comprehensive standard library, and the wide array of third-party libraries and frameworks. This capacity for rapid development and testing accelerates the innovation process, particularly in fast-evolving fields like AI and data science.

Ease of Use and Readability

At the core of Python's suitability for rapid prototyping is its ease of use and readability. Python's syntax is designed to be intuitive and clean, with a strong emphasis on readability, which reduces the cognitive load on developers. This allows for the quick translation of ideas into code, a crucial factor in rapid prototyping where the ability to iterate quickly is valuable. Python's straightforward syntax enables developers to focus on solving the problem at hand rather than wrestling with the language's complexities.

Comprehensive Standard Library and Third-Party Modules

Python's extensive standard library, often referred to as its "batteries included" feature, provides a wide array of modules and functions for common programming tasks. This comprehensive support minimizes the need for external dependencies and simplifies the implementation of a broad range of functionalities, from file I/O operations to network communication.

Furthermore, the Python ecosystem is enriched by a vast collection of third-party libraries and frameworks tailored for specific domains. In data science and AI, libraries like NumPy, Pandas, TensorFlow, and PyTorch offer high-level abstractions for complex operations, allowing for the rapid development and testing of models. For web development, frameworks like Django and Flask streamline the creation of web applications, from prototyping to deployment.

Interactive Development Environments

Python's support for interactive development environments (IDEs) and tools, such as Jupyter Notebooks, further enhances its rapid prototyping capabilities. Jupyter Notebooks, in particular, provide a versatile platform for exploratory coding, data analysis, and visualization, all within an interactive document. This interactivity enables a trial-and-error approach to coding, ideal for prototyping and experimentation. Developers and researchers can test new algorithms, visualize data, and refine models in real-time, significantly accelerating the development process.

Dynamic Typing and High-Level Data Structures

Python's dynamic typing system and high-level data structures contribute significantly to its rapid prototyping strengths. The dynamic typing allows variables to be declared without an explicit type, making the code more flexible and faster to write. High-level data structures like lists, dictionaries, and sets offer efficient and intuitive ways to store and manipulate data, essential for developing complex algorithms and applications swiftly.

Community Support and Resources

The global Python community plays a crucial role in the language's capacity for rapid prototyping. An active and supportive community means access to a wealth of knowledge, documentation, tutorials, and forums where developers can find answers and solutions quickly. The availability of open-source projects and code snippets provides a rich resource pool that developers can draw from, reducing development time by reusing and adapting existing solutions.

Python's design philosophy, comprehensive ecosystem, and the supportive global community collectively establish it as an excellent tool for rapid prototyping. Its ease of use, coupled with the extensive libraries and interactive tools, allows developers to quickly bring ideas to life, test hypotheses, and iterate on solutions. These capabilities not only streamline the development process but also foster innovation, making Python a key player in driving advancements across various technological and scientific domains.

Python's versatility and flexibility are key to its widespread adoption and acclaim. By catering to a broad spectrum of development needs, integrating seamlessly with other languages and technologies, and adapting to various programming paradigms, Python has established itself as a pivotal tool in the modern developer's toolkit. Whether for professional software development, academic research, or hobbyist projects, Python's capabilities make it uniquely positioned to address the challenges and opportunities of today's digital landscape.

Interpreted Nature:

Python is an interpreted language, which means that code execution occurs line by line, rather than being compiled into machine code beforehand. This interpretive nature makes Python well-suited for interactive development and rapid prototyping, allowing developers to test ideas, experiment with algorithms, and iterate quickly without the overhead of compilation. The interactive Python shell, commonly known as the REPL (Read-Eval-Print Loop), provides an immediate feedback loop that facilitates exploration and experimentation, making it an invaluable tool for AI development.

Immediate Execution

The interpreted nature of Python allows for immediate execution of code, which is particularly advantageous during the development process. Programmers can write a piece of code and run it instantly to see the results or debug errors without the need for a separate compilation step. This immediate feedback loop is invaluable for learning, experimentation, and debugging, enabling developers to understand the effects of their code changes in real-time.

Platform Independence

Python programs are executed by the Python interpreter, which is available for almost all operating systems, including Windows, macOS, Linux, and Unix, among others. This platform independence means that Python code can run on any system where the Python interpreter is installed, without the need to modify the code for different platforms. This cross-platform capability simplifies the development and deployment process, making Python an attractive option for developing portable applications.

Ease of Use and Learning

The interpreted nature of Python contributes to its overall ease of use and learning. Beginners find Python accessible because they can start experimenting with code snippets in an interactive shell or script without dealing with the complexities of compiling and linking that come with many compiled languages. This ease of experimentation and immediate validation of code encourages a more explorative learning process and a smoother introduction to programming concepts.

Dynamic Typing

Python's dynamic typing system is complemented by its interpreted nature. Variables in Python do not need to be declared with a specific data type, and types can change over the lifetime of a variable. This flexibility allows developers to write code more quickly and with fewer preliminary declarations, fostering a more agile development process. The ability to work with complex data types without extensive upfront definitions is particularly beneficial in fields like data science and AI, where data structures can be varied and complex.

Simplified Variable Declaration

In Python, variables do not require an explicit declaration to reserve memory space. The declaration happens automatically when a value is assigned to a variable, with the Python interpreter inferring the variable type. This means that programmers can write more intuitive and faster-to-code scripts, as they are not burdened by stringent type declarations. This simplicity is especially advantageous for beginners and for rapid prototyping, where the focus is on the logic and functionality rather than on detailed type management.

Flexibility in Data Types

Dynamic typing allows the type of a variable to change over its lifetime, providing a high degree of flexibility in handling data. This capability is particularly useful in AI and data science projects, where the nature of data can evolve as the data is processed. For instance, a variable initially holding an integer value can later store a string, a list, or even a complex object. This flexibility facilitates a more exploratory and iterative approach to development, enabling programmers to adapt their code easily as their data processing needs change.

Ease of Use and Readability

Python's dynamic typing contributes to the language's overall ease of use and readability. Without the clutter of explicit type declarations, Python code is cleaner and more straightforward, making it easier to read and understand. This readability is invaluable in collaborative projects and educational settings, where clear and accessible code is essential for effective teamwork and learning.

Duck Typing

Python employs a concept known as "duck typing," which is a subset of dynamic typing. Duck typing means that an object's suitability for a particular operation is determined by the presence of certain methods and properties, rather than by the type of the object itself. This approach allows for more flexible and generic code, enabling functions to operate on a variety of objects, as long as they have the right attributes or methods, hence the phrase "If it looks like a duck and quacks like a duck, it's a duck."

Performance Considerations

While dynamic typing offers significant flexibility and development speed, it can introduce performance overheads. The interpreter's need to determine types at runtime can slow down execution compared to statically typed languages, where types are known at compile time. However, for many applications, especially in scripting, data analysis, and rapid prototyping, the convenience and developer productivity gains outweigh the performance trade-offs.

Type Annotations and Checking

In response to the need for greater type safety and to leverage the advantages of static typing in certain contexts, Python 3 introduced type annotations. These annotations allow developers to hint at the data type of a variable, function parameter, or return value. While these annotations do not change Python's dynamic typing nature, they can be used with tools like MyPy for static type checking, offering a compromise between dynamic flexibility and static safety. This feature exemplifies Python's adaptability, catering to a broader range of programming styles and needs.

Dynamic typing is a cornerstone of Python's design philosophy, emphasizing ease of use, readability, and flexibility. It supports a broad spectrum of programming tasks, from simple scripts to complex AI models, making Python an appealing choice for developers across various disciplines. While it presents trade-offs in terms of performance, the productivity gains and the flexibility it affords, especially in data-centric fields, make Python an invaluable tool in the modern programming landscape.

Integration and Extensibility

The interpreted nature of Python makes it highly integrable with other programming languages and technologies. Python can easily invoke C/C++ libraries, and vice versa, allowing for the extension of Python applications with modules written in these languages for performance-critical tasks. This capability to integrate and extend makes Python a flexible choice for projects that require the high-level simplicity of Python but also need to leverage the performance benefits of compiled languages.

Scripting and Automation

Python is widely used for scripting and automation tasks due to its interpreted nature. Scripts written in Python can automate routine tasks, such as file management, data processing, and system administration, with minimal setup. The ability to write and execute scripts rapidly, without a compilation step, streamlines the process of developing automation scripts, making Python a popular choice for system administrators and DevOps professionals.

The interpreted nature of Python is a key feature that underpins its popularity and widespread use across various programming disciplines. It enhances Python's ease of use, promotes platform independence, facilitates learning, and supports rapid development and prototyping. Furthermore, it enables seamless integration with other languages and is ideal for scripting and automation tasks. These benefits collectively make Python a versatile and powerful tool for developers, researchers, and educators alike, driving its adoption in a wide array of applications from web development to cutting-edge research in AI.

Dynamic Typing:

Python is dynamically typed, meaning that variables are not explicitly declared with a data type and can change their type during runtime. This dynamic typing reduces the verbosity of code and enhances flexibility, allowing developers to write concise and expressive programs without the need for explicit type annotations. While dynamic typing introduces some potential pitfalls, such as type errors at runtime, Python's strong support for duck typing and runtime introspection mitigates these issues and promotes code reusability and extensibility.

Simplified Variable Declaration

In Python, variables do not require an explicit declaration to reserve memory space. The declaration happens automatically when a value is assigned to a variable, with the Python interpreter inferring the variable type. This means that programmers can write more intuitive and faster-to-code scripts, as they are not burdened by stringent type declarations. This simplicity is especially advantageous for beginners and for rapid prototyping, where the focus is on the logic and functionality rather than on detailed type management.

Flexibility in Data Types

Dynamic typing allows the type of a variable to change over its lifetime, providing a high degree of flexibility in handling data. This capability is particularly useful in AI and data science projects, where the nature of data can evolve as the data is processed. For instance, a variable initially holding an integer value can later store a string, a list, or even a complex object. This flexibility facilitates a more exploratory and iterative approach to development, enabling programmers to adapt their code easily as their data processing needs change.

Ease of Use and Readability

Python's dynamic typing contributes to the language's overall ease of use and readability. Without the clutter of explicit type declarations, Python code is cleaner and more straightforward, making it easier to read and understand. This readability is invaluable in collaborative projects and educational settings, where clear and accessible code is essential for effective teamwork and learning.

Duck Typing

Python employs a concept known as "duck typing," which is a subset of dynamic typing. Duck typing means that an object's suitability for a particular operation is determined by the presence of certain methods and properties, rather than by the type of the object itself. This approach allows for more flexible and generic code, enabling functions to operate on a variety of objects, as long as they have the right attributes or methods, hence the phrase "If it looks like a duck and quacks like a duck, it's a duck."

Performance Considerations

While dynamic typing offers significant flexibility and development speed, it can introduce performance overheads. The interpreter's need to determine types at runtime can slow down execution compared to statically typed languages, where types are known at compile time. However, for many applications, especially in scripting, data analysis, and rapid prototyping, the convenience and developer productivity gains outweigh the performance trade-offs.

Type Annotations and Checking

In response to the need for greater type safety and to leverage the advantages of static typing in certain contexts, Python 3 introduced type annotations. These annotations allow developers to hint at the data type of a variable, function parameter, or return value. While these annotations do not change Python's dynamic typing nature, they can be used with tools like MyPy for static type checking, offering a compromise between dynamic flexibility and static safety. This feature exemplifies Python's adaptability, catering to a broader range of programming styles and needs.

Dynamic typing is a cornerstone of Python's design philosophy, emphasizing ease of use, readability, and flexibility. It supports a broad spectrum of programming tasks, from simple scripts to complex AI models, making Python an appealing choice for developers across various disciplines. While it presents trade-offs in terms of performance, the productivity gains and the flexibility it affords, especially in data-centric fields, make Python an invaluable tool in the modern programming landscape.

Object-Oriented Paradigm:

Python is a multi-paradigm programming language that supports both procedural and object-oriented programming (OOP) paradigms. OOP is particularly well-suited for AI development, as it enables developers to model real-world entities as objects with properties and behaviors, facilitating modular and maintainable code design. Python's support for classes, inheritance, polymorphism, and encapsulation empowers developers to organize code logically, abstract complex systems, and build reusable components, which are essential for developing scalable and maintainable AI applications.

Encapsulation: Hiding Information

Encapsulation is a core principle of OOP that involves bundling the data (attributes) and methods (functions) that operate on the data into a single unit, known as a class. In Python, classes define the structure and behaviors of objects, serving as blueprints from which objects are created. Encapsulation allows for information hiding, a practice where internal details of a class are hidden from the outside to prevent external parts of the program from directly accessing and modifying the object's internal data.

Python implements encapsulation by allowing developers to define private attributes and methods within a class using underscores (_ or __) as prefixes. This mechanism doesn't enforce strict access control as seen in some other languages but serves as a convention to indicate that certain parts of the class are intended for internal use only. This convention respects the "we're all consenting adults here" philosophy, entrusting developers with the responsibility of class usage.

Inheritance: Extending Functionality

Inheritance allows a class to inherit attributes and methods from another class, promoting code reuse and the creation of hierarchical class structures. The class that inherits is known as the child or subclass, while the class being inherited from is the parent or superclass.

Python supports single and multiple inheritances, enabling a subclass to inherit from one or multiple superclasses, respectively.

This feature is particularly useful in creating a categorized model of objects that share common functionalities, allowing for the extension of base class functionalities in subclasses through method overriding. Python's support for inheritance simplifies the process of creating and managing related classes, facilitating a more organized and modular codebase.

Polymorphism: Leveraging Inheritance and Encapsulation

Polymorphism in OOP allows objects of different classes to be treated as objects of a common superclass. It is closely related to inheritance and encapsulation, enabling a unified interface through which objects can be accessed and manipulated. In Python, polymorphism allows methods to perform different operations based on the object it is acting upon, even if the interface remains consistent.

This capability is achieved through method overriding, where a subclass can provide a specific implementation of a method that is already defined in its superclass. This allows for flexibility and the dynamic binding of methods at runtime, making the code more general, flexible, and extensible.

Python's Approach to OOP

Python's approach to OOP is characterized by its simplicity and flexibility. Unlike languages that enforce strict OOP principles, Python allows developers to choose the extent to which they want to use OOP, supporting procedural and functional programming paradigms as well. This flexibility ensures that Python can be used effectively across various types of projects, from small scripts to large, complex systems.

Classes in Python are first-class objects, meaning they are treated like any other object in the language. This allows for dynamic modification of classes and objects at runtime, further enhancing Python's flexibility. Additionally, Python's built-in functions like **isinstance()** and **issubclass()** facilitate runtime inspection of objects and classes, supporting dynamic and reflective programming practices.

Everything is an Object

In Python, everything is treated as an object, from basic data types like integers and strings to functions, modules, and even classes themselves. This unified approach simplifies the language and makes it highly flexible, allowing for consistent behavior across all types. Such consistency ensures that developers can apply the same operations and principles across different entities, enhancing the language's intuitiveness and ease of use.

Class Definition and Instantiation

Defining classes in Python is straightforward, thanks to its clear and concise syntax. A class encapsulates data for creating objects, with attributes to store data and methods to define behavior. Python's class mechanism adds classes to the language with a minimum of new syntax and semantics, a testament to Python's principle of simplicity. Instantiation of these classes is just as straightforward, enabling objects to be created with customizable attributes right from the outset.

Dynamic Attribute Access and Method Calls

Python's dynamic nature shines in its OOP implementation, allowing for dynamic access to attributes and methods. Objects can have attributes added, removed, or modified at runtime, and methods can be dynamically invoked. This flexibility is powerful for dynamic application behavior but requires careful design to maintain clarity and prevent errors.

Inheritance and Polymorphism

Python supports single and multiple inheritances, enabling subclasses to inherit attributes and methods from one or more parent classes. This feature fosters code reusability and a hierarchical organization of classes. Python's polymorphism allows a unified interface to access methods of different classes, enabling functions to use objects of different classes through the same interface, as long as these classes share the same parent class or implement required methods. This is achieved without the need for complex typecasting or checking, aligning with Python's emphasis on simplicity.

Encapsulation with Public, Protected, and Private Attributes

While Python does not enforce strict access control, it adopts a convention-based approach to encapsulation, using underscores (_) to indicate protected attributes and double underscores (__) for private attributes. This mechanism provides a way to prevent accidental access and modification of data, adhering to the principle of encapsulation while maintaining the language's flexible nature.

First-class Objects

In Python, classes are first-class objects, meaning they can be created at runtime, assigned to variables, passed as arguments, or used in any place where an object is expected. This treats functions and classes alike, providing a high degree of programming flexibility and enabling meta-programming patterns that can dynamically alter program behavior.

Decorators for Method Modification

Decorators in Python provide a syntactically pleasing way to modify the behavior of functions and methods, such as class methods, static methods, and properties. This feature allows for the extension or alteration of method functionality without modifying the method's code directly, promoting cleaner and more maintainable code.

Python's approach to OOP exemplifies the language's commitment to simplicity, flexibility, and power. By treating everything as an object and providing a consistent and intuitive framework for encapsulation, inheritance, and polymorphism, Python facilitates the development of complex software in a more natural and efficient manner. This approach supports not only the rapid development of applications but also encourages a deeper understanding of OOP principles, making Python a valuable tool for both beginners and experienced developers in various domains.

Conclusion

Python's support for the object-oriented paradigm is a testament to its design as a versatile and powerful programming language. By enabling developers to leverage OOP concepts such as encapsulation, inheritance, and polymorphism, Python facilitates the development of well-organized, reusable, and scalable code. Whether for web development, data analysis, AI, or scientific computing, Python's OOP features contribute significantly to its efficacy and popularity among developers worldwide.

In summary, Python's simplicity, versatility, interpretive nature, dynamic typing, and support for object-oriented programming make it an ideal language for AI development. Its clean syntax, extensive standard library, and vibrant ecosystem of third-party packages provide developers with the tools and resources needed to tackle complex AI tasks effectively. In the subsequent chapters of this book, we'll delve deeper into Python programming for AI, covering essential concepts, techniques, libraries, and real-world applications to equip you with the knowledge and skills needed to excel in the field of artificial intelligence.

Python's Role in AI And Machine Learning:

Python has emerged as the predominant language for Artificial Intelligence (AI) and machine learning development, owing to its rich ecosystem of libraries, ease of use, and flexibility. In this comprehensive part, we'll explore Python's pivotal role in AI and machine learning, highlighting its significance, key libraries, and contributions to the advancement of AI technologies.

1. **Rich Ecosystem of Libraries:** Python boasts a vast ecosystem of libraries and frameworks specifically tailored for AI and machine learning development. Some of the most prominent libraries include:

   - **NumPy:** NumPy is a fundamental library for numerical computing in Python, providing support for multi-dimensional arrays, mathematical functions, and linear algebra operations. It serves as the building block for many other AI libraries and frameworks.

- **Pandas:** Pandas is a powerful library for data manipulation and analysis, offering data structures such as DataFrames and Series that simplify data handling and preprocessing tasks, crucial for machine learning workflows.
- **Scikit-learn:** Scikit-learn is a versatile machine learning library that provides a wide range of algorithms and tools for tasks such as classification, regression, clustering, and dimensionality reduction. It's renowned for its user-friendly API and extensive documentation, making it accessible to both beginners and experts.
- **TensorFlow and Keras:** TensorFlow is an open-source deep learning framework developed by Google, while Keras is a high-level neural networks API that runs on top of TensorFlow. Together, they enable developers to build and train deep learning models for a variety of tasks, including image recognition, natural language processing, and reinforcement learning.
- **PyTorch:** PyTorch is another popular deep learning framework known for its flexibility, dynamic computation graph, and intuitive interface. It's widely used in both research and production environments for developing cutting-edge AI models.

II. Accessibility and Ease of Use:

Python's simplicity and readability make it accessible to a wide range of developers, including beginners with no prior programming experience. Its intuitive syntax and extensive documentation lower the barrier to entry for AI and machine learning development, enabling newcomers to quickly grasp core concepts and start building AI applications.

Python's significance in the realms of Artificial Intelligence (AI) and machine learning extends beyond its technical capabilities; its accessibility and ease of use play a pivotal role in democratizing these fields. In this comprehensive part, we'll delve into how Python's accessibility and user-friendly nature contribute to its prominence in AI and machine learning development.

1. **Intuitive Syntax and Readability:** Python's syntax is renowned for its simplicity and readability, making it an ideal language for beginners and seasoned developers alike. Unlike more complex languages, Python's code resembles natural language, reducing the learning curve for newcomers to AI and machine learning. The intuitive syntax enables developers to focus on solving problems rather than wrestling with the intricacies of the language itself.

2. **Abundant Learning Resources:** Python's popularity in AI and machine learning has led to the proliferation of learning resources, including tutorials, online courses, documentation, and community forums. These resources cater to learners of all levels, providing step-by-step guidance, practical examples, and interactive exercises to reinforce concepts. Aspiring AI practitioners can easily find learning materials tailored to their specific interests and skill levels, accelerating their journey to proficiency in Python and AI.

3. **Interactive Development Environment:** Python's interactive development environment, facilitated by tools like Jupyter Notebooks and Google Colab, promotes exploration and experimentation in AI and machine learning. With these tools, developers can write code, execute it, visualize results, and iterate on their algorithms in real-time. The interactive nature of Python fosters a dynamic and iterative approach to AI development, enabling developers to quickly test hypotheses, debug code, and refine their models.

4. **Extensive Documentation and Support:** Python's extensive documentation and vibrant community support further enhance its accessibility for AI and machine learning practitioners. The

official Python documentation provides comprehensive guides, tutorials, and references covering every aspect of the language and its libraries. Additionally, online forums like Stack Overflow, Reddit, and specialized AI communities offer platforms for developers to seek help, share knowledge, and collaborate on projects. The wealth of documentation and community support ensures that developers have access to the resources they need to overcome challenges and make progress in their AI endeavors.

5. **Adoption by Educational Institutions:** Python's accessibility has made it a staple in educational institutions worldwide, where it is often used as the language of choice for teaching AI and machine learning concepts. Universities, coding bootcamps, and online learning platforms incorporate Python into their curriculum, exposing students to AI techniques and tools early in their academic journey. By familiarizing students with Python's intuitive syntax and powerful libraries, educational institutions empower the next generation of AI practitioners to tackle complex problems and drive innovation in the field.

Python's accessibility and ease of use play a critical role in democratizing AI and machine learning, enabling a diverse range of developers, researchers, students, and enthusiasts to participate in these fields. By providing an intuitive syntax, abundant learning resources, interactive development environments, extensive documentation, and widespread adoption in education, Python empowers individuals from all backgrounds to harness the power of AI and machine learning for solving real-world problems and shaping the future of technology.

III. Flexibility and Customizability:

Python's versatility allows developers to tailor AI solutions to their specific needs, whether it's experimenting with different algorithms, fine-tuning model parameters, or integrating AI capabilities into existing software systems. Its dynamic typing, high-level data structures, and object-oriented features promote code reusability, modularity, and extensibility, facilitating the development of scalable and maintainable AI applications.

Python's versatility and flexibility are key factors that contribute to its prominent role in the fields of Artificial Intelligence (AI) and machine learning. In this comprehensive part, we'll explore how Python's flexibility and customizability empower developers to tailor AI solutions to their specific needs and drive innovation in the domain.

1. **Adaptability to Diverse Needs:** Python's versatility enables developers to address a wide range of AI and machine learning challenges, from simple data analysis tasks to complex deep learning models. Whether you're working on image recognition, natural language processing, recommendation systems, or autonomous agents, Python provides the tools and libraries needed to tackle diverse problems effectively. Its extensive ecosystem of libraries, frameworks, and tools caters to different use cases and application domains, empowering developers to choose the most suitable tools for their projects.

2. **Dynamic Typing and Expressive Syntax:** Python's dynamic typing and expressive syntax promote code flexibility and adaptability, allowing developers to write concise and expressive code that is easy to understand and modify. Unlike statically typed languages, where variables must be explicitly declared with a fixed data type, Python allows variables to change their type dynamically during runtime, making it easier to work with heterogeneous data types and adapt to changing requirements. This dynamic nature of Python promotes code flexibility and reduces development time, enabling developers to experiment with different approaches and iterate quickly on their AI models.

3. **Extensibility and Integration:** Python's extensibility and integration capabilities make it easy to incorporate AI functionality into existing software systems and workflows. Whether you're building web applications, mobile apps, or enterprise solutions,

Python can seamlessly integrate with other programming languages, platforms, and technologies. Its interoperability with languages like C/C++, Java, and JavaScript allows developers to leverage existing code and libraries, speeding up development and reducing time to market. Additionally, Python's support for interfacing with hardware devices, databases, and web services facilitates the integration of AI capabilities into real-world applications and environments.

4. **Customizable Libraries and Frameworks:** Python's rich ecosystem of libraries and frameworks provides developers with customizable building blocks for developing AI solutions. Whether you're building a custom deep learning model from scratch or leveraging pre-trained models and algorithms, Python offers libraries like TensorFlow, Keras, PyTorch, and scikit-learn that can be customized and extended to meet specific requirements. These libraries provide a high level of abstraction, allowing developers to focus on solving higher-level problems without getting bogged down by low-level implementation details. Additionally, Python's open-source nature encourages community contributions and collaboration, resulting in a diverse range of libraries and tools that cater to different needs and preferences.

5. **Scalability and Performance:** Despite being an interpreted language, Python offers scalability and performance suitable for AI and machine learning applications. With libraries like NumPy, which provides efficient array operations and numerical computing capabilities, Python can handle large-scale data processing and computational tasks effectively. Additionally, Python's support for parallel processing, distributed computing, and GPU acceleration allows developers to scale their AI models and algorithms to handle increasingly large datasets and computational workloads.

Python's flexibility and customizability empower developers to build AI solutions that are tailored to their specific needs and requirements.

Whether you're a beginner exploring the basics of machine learning or an experienced practitioner building complex deep learning models, Python provides the tools, libraries, and flexibility needed to succeed in the dynamic and rapidly evolving field of AI and machine learning. In the subsequent chapters of this book, we'll delve deeper into Python programming for AI, covering essential concepts, techniques, libraries, and real-world applications to equip you with the knowledge and skills needed to excel in this exciting domain.

IV. Community Support and Collaboration:

Python's vibrant and active community of developers, researchers, and enthusiasts contributes to its continuous growth and evolution in the field of AI and machine learning. The open-source nature of Python fosters collaboration, knowledge sharing, and innovation, leading to the rapid development and adoption of new AI technologies and methodologies. Community-driven initiatives, such as online forums, tutorials, and open-source projects, provide invaluable resources and support to developers at all skill levels, enriching the ecosystem and advancing the state-of-the-art in AI.

Python's vibrant and supportive community plays a crucial role in its prominence in the fields of Artificial Intelligence (AI) and machine learning. In this comprehensive part, we'll explore how Python's community support and collaboration foster innovation, knowledge sharing, and collective growth in AI and machine learning development.

1. **Open-Source Philosophy:** Python's open-source philosophy underpins its thriving community and collaborative ecosystem. Python is developed and maintained by a global community of contributors who volunteer their time and expertise to improve the language and its associated libraries and frameworks. The open-source nature of Python encourages transparency, inclusivity, and participation, enabling developers from diverse backgrounds and skill levels to contribute to its development and evolution.

2. **Abundance of Learning Resources:** Python's community-driven ethos has led to the creation of a wealth of learning resources, including tutorials, documentation, blogs, videos, and online courses dedicated to AI and machine learning. These resources cater to learners of all levels, providing valuable insights, practical examples, and step-by-step guidance on Python programming, AI concepts, and machine learning techniques. Whether you're a beginner seeking to learn the basics or an experienced practitioner looking to deepen your knowledge, Python's community offers abundant resources to support your learning journey.

3. **Collaborative Platforms and Forums:** Python's community thrives on collaborative platforms and forums where developers can seek help, share knowledge, and collaborate on projects. Platforms like GitHub, GitLab, and Bitbucket host millions of open-source projects, including AI and machine learning libraries and frameworks, allowing developers to contribute code, report issues, and propose enhancements. Additionally, online forums and discussion boards like Stack Overflow, Reddit, and specialized AI communities provide spaces for developers to ask questions, exchange ideas, and engage in meaningful discussions about AI and machine learning topics.

4. **Contribution to Open-Source Projects:** Python's community actively contributes to the development of open-source AI and machine learning projects, driving innovation and advancing the state-of-the-art in the field. From developing new algorithms and models to improving existing libraries and frameworks, community members collaborate on a wide range of projects aimed at solving real-world problems and pushing the boundaries of AI research. The collaborative nature of open-source development fosters creativity, diversity, and inclusivity, ensuring that AI technologies are accessible and beneficial to all.

5. **Knowledge Sharing and Mentorship:** Python's community fosters a culture of knowledge sharing and mentorship, where experienced developers mentor newcomers, share best practices, and provide guidance on AI and machine learning development. Whether through online tutorials, workshops, hackathons, or mentorship programs, community members actively contribute to the learning and professional growth of others, creating opportunities for collaboration, networking, and skill development. By nurturing a supportive and inclusive community, Python empowers individuals from all backgrounds to succeed in AI and machine learning.

Python's community support and collaboration are essential pillars of its success in the fields of AI and machine learning. Through open-source contributions, abundant learning resources, collaborative platforms, and knowledge sharing initiatives, Python's community fosters innovation, inclusivity, and collective growth, driving progress and advancements in AI research and development. As you embark on your journey into Python for AI, you'll find a welcoming and supportive community ready to help you learn, grow, and succeed in this exciting and dynamic domain.

In summary, Python's rich ecosystem of libraries, accessibility, flexibility, and community support make it the language of choice for AI and machine learning development. Whether you're a beginner exploring the basics of machine learning or an experienced practitioner building sophisticated deep learning models, Python provides the tools, resources, and community-driven momentum needed to drive innovation and make meaningful contributions to the field of artificial intelligence. In the subsequent chapters of this book, we'll delve deeper into Python programming for AI, covering essential concepts, techniques, libraries, and real-world applications to equip you with the knowledge and skills needed to excel in the exciting and dynamic field of AI and machine learning.

Setting Up Python Development Environment:

Before delving into Python for Artificial Intelligence (AI), it's crucial to set up a robust development environment that facilitates smooth coding, experimentation, and testing. In this comprehensive part, we'll explore the essential steps to set up a Python development environment tailored for AI and machine learning projects.

1. Installing Python:

The first step in setting up your Python development environment is to install Python itself. Python is available for multiple platforms, including Windows, macOS, and Linux, and can be downloaded from the official Python website (python.org). It's recommended to install the latest version of Python to access the newest features and improvements.

Installing Python is the foundational step in setting up your development environment for AI and machine learning projects. Python is the primary programming language used in these fields due to its simplicity, versatility, and extensive ecosystem of libraries and frameworks. In this comprehensive part, we'll explore the process of installing Python on different platforms to kickstart your journey into AI development.

1. Installing Python on Windows:

- Visit the official Python website (python.org) and navigate to the downloads section.
- Choose the latest version of Python for Windows and download the installer (either the executable installer or the web-based installer).
- Run the installer and follow the prompts to install Python on your system. Make sure to check the option to add Python to PATH during installation.

- Once the installation is complete, you can verify the installation by opening Command Prompt and running the command **python --version**.

2. Installing Python on macOS:

- macOS typically comes with Python pre-installed. However, it's recommended to install the latest version of Python for development purposes.
- Visit the official Python website (python.org) and navigate to the downloads section.
- Choose the latest version of Python for macOS and download the installer (either the macOS 64-bit installer or the macOS 64-bit Intel installer).
- Run the installer and follow the prompts to install Python on your system.
- Once the installation is complete, you can verify the installation by opening Terminal and running the command **python --version**.

3. Installing Python on Linux:

- Most Linux distributions come with Python pre-installed. However, you may need to install additional Python packages and development tools.
- Use your distribution's package manager (e.g., apt for Ubuntu, yum for CentOS) to install Python. For example, on Ubuntu, you can install Python 3 by running the command **sudo apt-get install python3**.
- You can also install Python from source by downloading the source code from the official Python website and following the instructions in the README file.

4. Managing Python Versions:

- If you need to work with multiple versions of Python simultaneously, consider using a version management tool like pyenv (for macOS and Linux) or pyenv-win (for Windows).
- These tools allow you to install and switch between different Python versions easily, ensuring compatibility with various projects and dependencies.

5. Using Python Distribution Bundles:

- Alternatively, you can use Python distribution bundles like Anaconda or Miniconda, which come pre-packaged with Python and essential libraries for data science and machine learning.
- Anaconda provides a user-friendly package manager called conda, which allows you to manage Python environments, install packages, and create virtual environments with ease.

In summary, installing Python is a straightforward process that lays the foundation for your AI and machine learning development journey. By following the steps outlined above, you'll have Python up and running on your system, ready to explore the vast world of AI libraries, frameworks, and tools that Python has to offer.

II. Choosing a Code Editor or Integrated Development Environment (IDE):

Once Python is installed, you'll need a code editor or Integrated Development Environment (IDE) to write and execute Python code effectively. Popular choices include:

Visual Studio Code: A lightweight and versatile code editor with excellent Python support, including syntax highlighting, code completion, and debugging capabilities.

Selecting an appropriate code editor or Integrated Development Environment (IDE) is crucial for efficient Python development, especially in the context of Artificial Intelligence (AI) projects. Visual Studio Code (VS Code) stands out as a popular choice among developers due to its versatility, robust features, and extensive support for Python development. In this comprehensive part, we'll explore how to set up Visual Studio Code for Python development, enabling you to kickstart your journey into AI programming.

1. **Installing Visual Studio Code:**

- Visual Studio Code is a free and open-source code editor developed by Microsoft, available for Windows, macOS, and Linux.
- Visit the official Visual Studio Code website (code.visualstudio.com) and download the installer for your operating system.
- Run the installer and follow the on-screen instructions to install Visual Studio Code on your system.

2. **Installing Python Extension for Visual Studio Code:**

- Once Visual Studio Code is installed, launch the application.
- Open the Extensions view by clicking on the Extensions icon in the Activity Bar on the side of the window or by pressing **Ctrl+Shift+X**.
- Search for "Python" in the Extensions view and install the official Python extension developed by Microsoft.
- This extension provides features such as IntelliSense (code completion), linting, debugging, code formatting, and Jupyter notebook support for Python development in Visual Studio Code.

3. **Configuring Python Interpreter:**

- After installing the Python extension, you'll need to configure the Python interpreter for your project.
- Open your Python project folder in Visual Studio Code or create a new Python file.

- Press **Ctrl+Shift+P** to open the command palette, then type "Python: Select Interpreter" and press Enter.
- Choose the desired Python interpreter from the list of available interpreters installed on your system.
- This step ensures that Visual Studio Code uses the correct Python interpreter for running your Python scripts and executing code.

4. Using Visual Studio Code Features:

- Visual Studio Code offers a wide range of features to enhance your Python development experience.
- IntelliSense provides intelligent code completion, suggesting variable names, function definitions, and module imports as you type.
- Linting detects errors and potential issues in your code, high-lighting them with squiggly lines and providing suggestions for fixes.
- Debugging allows you to set breakpoints, inspect variables, and step through your code line by line to identify and fix bugs.
- Code formatting automatically formats your code according to predefined style guidelines, ensuring consistency and readability.

5. Exploring Additional Extensions:

- Visual Studio Code supports a variety of extensions that can further enhance your Python development workflow.
- You can install additional extensions for specific tasks such as version control (e.g., Git), code snippets, Docker integration, and more, depending on your project requirements.

In summary, setting up Visual Studio Code for Python development provides a powerful and versatile environment for building AI applications. By following the steps outlined above and leveraging Visual Studio Code's features and extensions, you'll be well-equipped to tackle AI projects with confidence and efficiency.

- **PyCharm:** A powerful Python IDE developed by JetBrains, offering advanced features such as code analysis, refactoring, and integrated version control.
- **Jupyter Notebook:** An interactive computing environment that allows you to create and share documents containing live code, visualizations, and narrative text. Jupyter Notebook is particularly well-suited for data analysis, prototyping, and exploratory research in AI and machine learning.

III. Installing Required Libraries and Frameworks:

Python's strength in AI and machine learning stems from its rich ecosystem of libraries and frameworks. Depending on your specific AI project requirements, you may need to install additional libraries such as:

- **NumPy:** A fundamental library for numerical computing in Python, providing support for multi-dimensional arrays, mathematical functions, and linear algebra operations.
- **Pandas:** A powerful library for data manipulation and analysis, offering data structures such as DataFrames and Series that simplify data handling and preprocessing tasks.
- **TensorFlow and Keras:** Popular deep learning frameworks for building and training neural networks, with TensorFlow providing low-level control and Keras offering high-level abstractions and simplicity.
- **scikit-learn:** A versatile machine learning library that provides a wide range of algorithms and tools for tasks such as classification, regression, clustering, and dimensionality reduction.

You can install these libraries using Python's package manager, pip, by running commands like **pip install numpy**, **pip install pandas**, **pip install tensorflow**, etc., in your command-line interface.

IV. Setting up Virtual Environments:

To manage dependencies and ensure project isolation, it's recommended to set up virtual environments for your Python projects. Virtual environments allow you to install project-specific packages without affecting the system-wide Python installation. You can create a virtual environment using the **venv** module (for Python 3) or **virtualenv** package (for Python 2 and 3) and activate it using commands like **source venv/bin/activate** (on macOS/Linux) or **venv\Scripts\ activate** (on Windows).

Virtual environments are essential for managing dependencies and isolating project-specific packages in Python development, particularly in the context of Artificial Intelligence (AI) projects where different projects may require different sets of dependencies. In this comprehensive part, we'll explore how to set up virtual environments for Python development, enabling you to create isolated environments for your AI projects.

1. **Installing Virtual Environment Tool:**

- Python comes with a built-in module called **venv** (for Python 3) or **virtualenv** (for Python 2 and 3) for creating virtual environments.
- If you're using Python 3, the **venv** module is included by default, and you can create virtual environments using the **python3 -m venv <env_name>** command.
- If you're using Python 2 or need additional features, you can install the **virtualenv** package using pip: **pip install virtualenv**.

2. **Creating a Virtual Environment:**

- Once you have the virtual environment tool installed, navigate to your project directory using the command-line interface (CLI).
- Run the command **python -m venv <env_name>** (for Python 3) or **virtualenv <env_name>** (for Python 2 or with the **virtualenv** package installed) to create a new virtual environment.
- Replace **<env_name>** with the desired name for your virtual environment. This will create a new directory with the specified name containing the virtual environment files.

3. Activating the Virtual Environment:

- After creating the virtual environment, you need to activate it to start using it for your project.
- On Windows, activate the virtual environment by running the command **<env_name>\Scripts\activate**.
- On macOS and Linux, activate the virtual environment by running the command **source <env_name>/bin/activate**.
- Once activated, the name of the virtual environment will appear in parentheses at the beginning of the command prompt, indicating that you are now working within the virtual environment.

4. Installing Dependencies:

- With the virtual environment activated, you can now install project-specific dependencies using pip.
- Run **pip install <package_name>** to install individual packages or **pip install -r requirements.txt** to install packages listed in a requirements file (**requirements.txt**).
- These packages will be installed within the virtual environment, ensuring that they are isolated from other Python installations and projects.

5. Deactivating the Virtual Environment:

- When you're done working on your project, you can deactivate the virtual environment to return to the global Python environment.
- Simply run the command **deactivate** in the CLI, and the virtual environment will be deactivated.

6. Managing Multiple Virtual Environments:

- If you're working on multiple projects with different dependencies, it's recommended to create a separate virtual environment for each project.
- By maintaining separate virtual environments for each project, you can avoid conflicts between dependencies and ensure project isolation.

Setting up virtual environments is essential for Python development, particularly in AI projects where managing dependencies is crucial. By following the steps outlined above, you can create isolated environments for your AI projects, allowing you to manage dependencies effectively and ensure project consistency and reproducibility.

V. Exploring Cloud Platforms:

For more advanced AI projects and collaborative work, consider exploring cloud-based development platforms such as Google Colab, Microsoft Azure Notebooks, or Amazon SageMaker. These platforms offer pre-configured environments with access to powerful hardware accelerators (e.g., GPUs, TPUs) and a range of AI and machine learning tools and services, making them ideal for large-scale experimentation and production deployments.

In addition to local development environments, exploring cloud platforms for Python development can offer several advantages, particularly for AI and machine learning projects. Cloud platforms provide access to powerful computing resources, scalable infrastructure, and specialized AI services, enabling developers to accelerate development, experimentation, and deployment. In this comprehensive part, we'll explore how to leverage cloud platforms for Python development in AI projects.

1. Google Colab:

- Google Colab is a free, cloud-based Jupyter notebook environment that allows you to write and execute Python code directly in your web browser.
- Colab provides access to Google's powerful computing infrastructure, including GPUs and TPUs, enabling you to train deep learning models at scale without the need for expensive hardware.
- You can import datasets from Google Drive, install additional Python libraries using pip, and collaborate with others in real-time.
- Colab notebooks can be saved to Google Drive or exported in various formats for sharing and collaboration.

2. Microsoft Azure Notebooks:

- Azure Notebooks is a free cloud service provided by Microsoft Azure that allows you to create and run Jupyter notebooks in the cloud.
- Azure Notebooks provides access to a wide range of Python libraries and frameworks, including Azure Machine Learning SDK for building and deploying machine learning models.
- You can choose from different runtime environments, including Python 2, Python 3, and R, and select compute resources based on your requirements.

- Azure Notebooks integrates with other Azure services, such as Azure Storage and Azure Machine Learning, for data storage, processing, and model deployment.

3. Amazon SageMaker:

- Amazon SageMaker is a fully managed machine learning service provided by Amazon Web Services (AWS) that allows you to build, train, and deploy machine learning models at scale.
- SageMaker provides a comprehensive set of tools and features for every step of the machine learning workflow, from data pre-processing and model training to deployment and monitoring.
- You can choose from built-in algorithms and frameworks or bring your own custom algorithms and Docker containers.
- SageMaker integrates with other AWS services, such as S3 for data storage, IAM for access control, and CloudWatch for monitoring and logging.

4. IBM Watson Studio:

- IBM Watson Studio is an integrated development environment (IDE) provided by IBM Watson that allows you to build and deploy AI and machine learning models in the cloud.
- Watson Studio provides a collaborative environment for data scientists, developers, and domain experts to work together on AI projects.
- You can choose from a variety of tools and services, including Jupyter notebooks, RStudio, and visual modeling tools, to analyze data, build models, and deploy applications.
- Watson Studio integrates with other IBM Watson services, such as Watson Machine Learning for model deployment, Watson Discovery for natural language processing, and Watson Assistant for building conversational AI solutions.

5. Benefits of Cloud Platforms for Python Development:

- Scalability: Cloud platforms offer scalable infrastructure and computing resources, allowing you to scale your AI projects to handle large datasets and complex computations.
- Accessibility: Cloud platforms provide access to computing resources from anywhere with an internet connection, enabling remote collaboration and flexibility in development.
- Cost-effectiveness: Cloud platforms offer pay-as-you-go pricing models, allowing you to pay only for the resources you use and avoid upfront hardware costs.
- Specialized AI Services: Cloud platforms offer specialized AI services, such as natural language processing, computer vision, and speech recognition, that can be easily integrated into your Python projects.

Exploring cloud platforms for Python development can provide several benefits for AI and machine learning projects, including access to powerful computing resources, scalable infrastructure, and specialized AI services. By leveraging cloud platforms like Google Colab, Microsoft Azure Notebooks, Amazon SageMaker, and IBM Watson Studio, you can accelerate development, experimentation, and deployment of AI solutions while reducing infrastructure overhead and costs.Top of Form

In summary, setting up a Python development environment for AI and machine learning involves installing Python, choosing a code editor or IDE, installing required libraries and frameworks, setting up virtual environments for project isolation, and exploring cloud platforms for advanced capabilities. By following these steps, you'll create a robust and efficient development environment that empowers you to tackle AI projects with confidence and efficiency.

Chapter 2: Python Basics

Python Basics

Python is a high-level, interpreted programming language known for its simplicity, readability, and versatility. In this comprehensive part, we'll cover the fundamental concepts and syntax of Python, laying the groundwork for understanding more advanced topics in Python programming.

1. **Variables and Data Types:**

- In Python, variables are used to store data values. You can assign a value to a variable using the assignment operator =. For example, **x = 5**.
- Python supports various data types, including integers, floats, strings, booleans, lists, tuples, dictionaries, and sets. You can dynamically assign data types to variables without explicitly declaring them.

2. **Control Flow Statements:**

- Python provides several control flow statements, including if-else statements, for loops, while loops, and try-except blocks.
- If-else statements allow you to execute different code blocks based on specified conditions. For example:

```
if x > 0:
print("Positive")
elif x < 0:
print("Negative")
else:
print("Zero")
```

- For loops iterate over a sequence (e.g., lists, tuples, strings) and execute a block of code for each element. While loops repeatedly execute a block of code as long as a specified condition is true.

3. Functions:

- Functions in Python are reusable blocks of code that perform a specific task. You can define functions using the **def** keyword followed by the function name and parameters. For example:

```
def greet(name):
print("Hello, " + name + "!")
```

- You can call a function by using its name followed by parentheses and passing arguments if required. For example: **greet("Alice")**.

4. Lists, Tuples, and Dictionaries:

- Lists are ordered collections of elements, which can be of different data types. You can modify lists by adding, removing, or modifying elements.
- Tuples are similar to lists but are immutable, meaning their elements cannot be changed after creation.
- Dictionaries are collections of key-value pairs, where each key is associated with a value. Dictionaries are unordered, and you can access values using keys.

5. File Handling:

- Python allows you to read from and write to files using file handling operations. You can open a file using the **open()** function, read or write data to the file, and close the file using the **close()** method.
- For example, to read from a file:

```
file = open("example.txt", "r")
contents = file.read()
print(contents)
file.close()
```

6. Object-Oriented Programming (OOP):

- Python supports object-oriented programming (OOP) concepts, including classes, objects, inheritance, encapsulation, and polymorphism.
- You can define classes using the **class** keyword, create objects (instances) of a class, and access object attributes and methods.

7. Libraries and Modules:

- Python has a vast ecosystem of libraries and modules that extend its functionality for various purposes, including data analysis, machine learning, web development, and more.
- You can import libraries and modules into your Python scripts using the **import** statement. For example: **import math, import numpy as np**.

In summary, understanding Python basics is essential for mastering Python programming and building AI applications. By grasping concepts such as variables, control flow statements, functions, data structures, file handling, object-oriented programming, and libraries, you'll have a solid foundation for developing Python-based AI solutions and exploring more advanced topics in the field.

Variables, Data Types, and Operators:

Understanding variables, data types, and operators is fundamental to mastering Python programming. In this comprehensive part, we'll explore these concepts in detail, providing explanations and examples to solidify your understanding.

1. **Variables:** Variables in Python are used to store data values. They act as placeholders that can be assigned different values throughout the program's execution. Here's how you can declare and use variables in Python:

   ```python
   # Variable assignment
   x = 10
   name = "Alice"
   is_valid = True
   # Variable reassignment
   x = 20
   name = "Bob"
   is_valid = False
   # Printing variables
   print(x) # Output: 20
   print(name) # Output: Bob
   print(is_valid) # Output: False
   ```

2. **Data Types:** Python supports various data types, each serving a specific purpose. Understanding data types is crucial for performing operations and manipulations on data. Here are some commonly used data types in Python:

- **Integer:** Whole numbers without decimal points.
- **Float:** Real numbers with decimal points.

- **String:** Sequence of characters enclosed within single or double quotes.
- **Boolean:** Logical values representing True or False.

```python
# Integer
x = 10
# Float
y = 3.14
# String
name = "Alice"
# Boolean
is_valid = True
```

3. Operators: Operators in Python are symbols or keywords used to perform operations on variables and values. Python supports various types of operators, including arithmetic, assignment, comparison, logical, and bitwise operators. Let's explore some examples of each type:

- **Arithmetic Operators:**

```python
a = 10
b = 5
print(a + b) # Addition: 15
print(a - b) # Subtraction: 5
print(a * b) # Multiplication: 50
print(a / b) # Division: 2.0
print(a % b) # Modulus: 0
print(a ** b) # Exponentiation: 100000
print(a // b) # Floor Division: 2
```

- **Assignment Operators:**

```python
x = 10
x += 5 # Equivalent to x = x + 5
x -= 3 # Equivalent to x = x - 3
```

```python
x *= 2 # Equivalent to x = x * 2
x /= 4 # Equivalent to x = x / 4
```

- **Comparison Operators:**

```python
a = 10
b = 5
print(a == b) # Equal to: False
print(a != b) # Not equal to: True
print(a > b) # Greater than: True
print(a < b) # Less than: False
print(a >= b) # Greater than or equal to: True
print(a <= b) # Less than or equal to: False
```

Logical Operators:

```python
x = True
y = False
print(x and y) # Logical AND: False
print(x or y) # Logical OR: True
print(not x) # Logical NOT: False
```

Bitwise Operators:

```python
a = 10
b = 5
print(a & b) # Bitwise AND: 0
print(a | b) # Bitwise OR: 15
print(a ^ b) # Bitwise XOR: 15
print(~a) # Bitwise NOT: -11
print(a << 1) # Bitwise Left Shift: 20
print(a >> 1) # Bitwise Right Shift: 2
```

By understanding variables, data types, and operators, you'll have a solid foundation in Python programming, enabling you to perform various operations and manipulations on data efficiently.

Control flow:

Control flow statements in Python allow you to control the flow of execution in your program based on certain conditions. Understanding if statements, loops, and conditional expressions is crucial for writing effective and structured Python code. Let's explore each of these concepts in detail:

1. **If Statements:**

   If statements are used to execute a block of code if a specified condition is true. They can also be accompanied by else and elif (else if) clauses to handle alternative conditions.

   ```python
   # Example of a simple if statement
   x = 10
   if x > 5:
   print("x is greater than 5")
   ```

   You can also use elif and else clauses to handle multiple conditions:

   ```python
   # Example of if-elif-else statement
   x = 10
   if x > 10:
   print("x is greater than 10")
   elif x == 10:
   print("x is equal to 10")
   else:
   print("x is less than 10")
   ```

2. **Loops:**

Loops are used to iterate over a sequence of elements or execute a block of code repeatedly until a specified condition is met. Python supports two main types of loops: for loops and while loops.

- **For Loops:**

For loops iterate over a sequence (e.g., lists, tuples, strings) and execute a block of code for each element in the sequence.

```
# Example of a for loop iterating over a list
fruits = ["apple", "banana", "cherry"]
for fruit in fruits:
print(fruit)
```

- **While Loops:**

While loops repeatedly execute a block of code as long as a specified condition is true.

```
# Example of a while loop
i = 1
while i <= 5:
print(i)
i += 1
```

3. Conditional Expressions:

Conditional expressions, also known as ternary operators, provide a concise way to write if-else statements in a single line.

```
# Example of a conditional expression
x = 10
result = "x is greater than 5" if x > 5 else "x is less than or equal to 5"
print(result)
```

4. Break and Continue Statements:

Python also provides break and continue statements to control the flow of loops.

- **Break Statement:** Terminates the loop prematurely when a certain condition is met.

```
# Example of a break statement
fruits = ["apple", "banana", "cherry"]
for fruit in fruits:
```

```
if fruit == "banana":
break
print(fruit)
```

Continue Statement: Skips the remaining code in the loop and moves to the next iteration when a certain condition is met.

```
# Example of a continue statement
fruits = ["apple", "banana", "cherry"]
for fruit in fruits:
if fruit == "banana":
continue
print(fruit)
```

By mastering if statements, loops, and conditional expressions, you'll gain greater control over the flow of your Python programs, enabling you to write more dynamic and efficient code for various tasks and applications.

Functions And Modules:

Functions and modules are essential concepts in Python programming that promote code organization, reusability, and modularity. Understanding how to define and use functions, as well as how to work with modules, is fundamental to writing clean and maintainable Python code. Let's delve into these concepts in detail:

1. **Functions:**

    Functions are blocks of reusable code that perform a specific task or operation. They allow you to break down complex tasks into smaller, manageable units, improving code readability and maintainability. In Python, you can define functions using the **def** keyword, followed by the function name and parameters (if any).

    ```
    # Example of a simple function
    ```

```python
def greet(name):
"""This function greets the user."""
print("Hello, " + name + "!")
```

Function Parameters: Parameters are variables that are passed to a function when it is called. They allow functions to accept input values and perform operations based on those values.

```python
# Example of a function with parameters
def add_numbers(x, y):
"""This function adds two numbers."""
return x + y
result = add_numbers(5, 3)
print("Result:", result) # Output: 8
```

Return Statement: The **return** statement is used to return a value from a function. It specifies the result or output of the function, which can then be used or stored for further processing.

```python
# Example of a function with a return statement
def square(x):
"""This function returns the square of a number."""
return x ** 2
result = square(4)
print("Square:", result) # Output: 16
```

2. **Modules:**

Modules in Python are files that contain Python code, including functions, classes, and variables. They allow you to organize related code into separate files and promote code reuse across multiple projects. You can create your own modules or use built-in modules provided by Python's standard library.

Creating Modules: To create a module, simply save your Python code in a **.py** file with a valid Python filename. You can then import the module into your Python scripts using the **import** statement.

```python
# Example of a module named mymodule.py
def greet(name):
```

```
"""This function greets the user."""
print("Hello, " + name + "!")
# Importing the module
import mymodule
mymodule.greet("Alice") # Output: Hello, Alice!
```

Using Built-in Modules: Python's standard library includes a wide range of built-in modules that provide ready-to-use functionality for various tasks, such as math operations, file I/O, and network communication. You can import and use these modules in your Python scripts.

```
# Example of using the math module
import math
result = math.sqrt(16)
print("Square root:", result) # Output: 4.0
```

Aliasing Modules: You can alias modules to provide shorter and more concise names when importing them. This can improve code readability, especially when dealing with long module names.

```
# Example of aliasing a module
import math as m
result = m.sqrt(25)
print("Square root:", result) # Output: 5.0
```

Importing Specific Functions: If you only need specific functions from a module, you can import them individually using the **from ... import** syntax.

```
# Example of importing specific functions from a module
from math import sqrt
result = sqrt(36)
print("Square root:", result) # Output: 6.0
```

By mastering functions and modules, you'll be able to write modular, reusable, and maintainable Python code, facilitating efficient development and collaboration across projects.

Chapter 3: Data Handling and Manipulation

Data handling and manipulation are essential skills for any Python programmer, especially in the realm of data science, machine learning, and artificial intelligence. Python offers powerful libraries and built-in data structures that facilitate the handling, manipulation, and analysis of data. In this comprehensive part, we'll explore various techniques and tools for data handling and manipulation, along with examples to illustrate their usage.

1. **Built-in Data Structures:**

   Python provides several built-in data structures for storing and organizing data, including lists, tuples, dictionaries, sets, and strings. Understanding how to work with these data structures is crucial for data manipulation tasks.

   Lists: Ordered collections of elements, mutable (modifiable), and can contain elements of different data types.

   # Example of a list

   fruits = ["apple", "banana", "cherry"]

   Tuples: Ordered collections of elements, immutable (unchangeable), and can contain elements of different data types.

   # Example of a tuple

   coordinates = (3, 5)

   Dictionaries: Unordered collections of key-value pairs, mutable, and keys must be unique.

```
# Example of a dictionary
person = {"name": "Alice", "age": 30}
```

Sets: Unordered collections of unique elements, mutable, and can perform set operations (e.g., union, intersection).

```
# Example of a set
numbers = {1, 2, 3, 4, 5}
```

2. **NumPy:**

NumPy is a powerful library for numerical computing in Python, providing support for large, multi-dimensional arrays and matrices, along with a collection of mathematical functions to operate on these arrays efficiently.

```
import numpy as np
# Example of creating a NumPy array
arr = np.array([1, 2, 3, 4, 5])
```

3. **Pandas:**

Pandas is a versatile library for data manipulation and analysis in Python, built on top of NumPy. It provides high-performance, easy-to-use data structures and functions for reading, writing, and manipulating structured data.

```
import pandas as pd
# Example of creating a DataFrame from a dictionary
data = {"Name": ["Alice", "Bob", "Charlie"],
"Age": [30, 25, 35]}
df = pd.DataFrame(data)
```

4. **Data Input and Output:**

Python offers various methods and libraries for reading data from external sources (e.g., files, databases) and writing data to different formats (e.g., CSV, Excel).

```
# Example of reading data from a CSV file using Pandas
df = pd.read_csv("data.csv")
# Example of writing data to a CSV file using Pandas
df.to_csv("output.csv", index=False)
```

5. **Data Manipulation:**

Once data is loaded into Python, you can perform various manipulations and transformations on it using functions and methods provided by libraries like NumPy and Pandas.

```
# Example of filtering data using Pandas
filtered_df = df[df["Age"] > 30]
# Example of adding a new column to a DataFrame
df["City"] = ["New York", "Los Angeles", "Chicago"]
```

6. **Data Visualization:**

Data visualization is an essential aspect of data analysis, allowing you to explore and communicate insights from data effectively. Python offers several libraries, such as Matplotlib and Seaborn, for creating various types of plots and charts.

```
import matplotlib.pyplot as plt
# Example of creating a bar plot using Matplotlib
plt.bar(df["Name"], df["Age"])
plt.xlabel("Name")
plt.ylabel("Age")
plt.title("Age Distribution")
plt.show()
```

By mastering data handling and manipulation techniques in Python, you'll be well-equipped to work with diverse datasets, perform complex analyses, and derive meaningful insights from data for various applications.

Working With Data Structures:

Data structures such as lists, tuples, dictionaries, and sets are fundamental to data handling and manipulation tasks in Python. They provide versatile ways to store, organize, and manipulate data efficiently. Let's explore each of these data structures in detail, along with examples to illustrate their usage:

1. **Lists:**

   Lists are ordered collections of elements, allowing for flexible and dynamic storage of data. They are mutable, meaning their elements can be modified after creation.

   ```python
   # Example of creating a list
   fruits = ["apple", "banana", "cherry"]
   ```

   Lists support various operations, including appending, extending, inserting, removing, and slicing elements:

   ```python
   # Example of list operations
   # Appending an element to the list
   fruits.append("orange")
   # Extending the list with another list
   more_fruits = ["grape", "kiwi"]
   fruits.extend(more_fruits)
   # Inserting an element at a specific position
   fruits.insert(2, "mango")
   # Removing an element from the list
   fruits.remove("banana")
   # Slicing the list to get a subset of elements
   subset = fruits[1:4]
   print(fruits) # Output: ['apple', 'cherry', 'mango', 'orange', 'grape', 'kiwi']
   print(subset) # Output: ['cherry', 'mango', 'orange']
   ```

2. **Tuples:**

   Tuples are ordered collections of elements, similar to lists, but they are immutable, meaning their elements cannot be modified after creation.

   ```python
   # Example of creating a tuple
   coordinates = (3, 5)
   ```

   Tuples are often used for representing fixed collections of values, such as coordinates, and for returning multiple values from functions.

   ```python
   # Example of using a tuple to return multiple values from a
   function
   ```

```python
def divide_and_remainder(dividend, divisor):
quotient = dividend // divisor
remainder = dividend % divisor
return quotient, remainder
result = divide_and_remainder(10, 3)
print("Quotient:", result[0])
print("Remainder:", result[1])
```

3. **Dictionaries:**

Dictionaries are unordered collections of key-value pairs, providing efficient lookup and storage of data. They are mutable and can store heterogeneous data types.

```python
# Example of creating a dictionary
person = {"name": "Alice", "age": 30, "city": "New York"}
```

Dictionaries support various operations, including accessing, adding, updating, and removing elements:

```python
# Example of dictionary operations
# Accessing values by key
print("Name:", person["name"])
print("Age:", person["age"])
# Adding a new key-value pair
person["email"] = "alice@example.com"
# Updating the value of an existing key
person["age"] = 31
# Removing a key-value pair
del person["city"]
print(person)  # Output: {'name': 'Alice', 'age': 31, 'email': 'alice@example.com'}
```

4. **Sets:**

Sets are unordered collections of unique elements, allowing for efficient membership testing and set operations such as union, intersection, and difference.

```python
# Example of creating a set
unique_numbers = {1, 2, 3, 4, 5}
```

Sets support various set operations, including adding, removing, and testing for membership:

```
# Example of set operations
# Adding an element to the set
unique_numbers.add(6)
# Removing an element from the set
unique_numbers.remove(3)
# Testing for membership
is_present = 5 in unique_numbers
print(unique_numbers) # Output: {1, 2, 4, 5, 6}
print(is_present) # Output: True
```

By mastering these data structures and their associated operations, you'll gain the ability to efficiently handle and manipulate data in Python, enabling you to tackle a wide range of data processing tasks effectively.

Introduction to Numpy:

NumPy is a fundamental library for numerical computing in Python. It provides support for large, multi-dimensional arrays and matrices, along with a collection of mathematical functions to operate on these arrays efficiently. In data handling and manipulation tasks, NumPy offers powerful tools for working with numerical data, enabling faster computation and manipulation compared to built-in Python lists. Let's explore NumPy in detail, along with examples to illustrate its usage:

1. **Installation:**

    Before using NumPy, you need to install it. You can install NumPy using pip, Python's package manager:
    ```
    pip install numpy
    ```
2. **Basics of NumPy Arrays:**

NumPy's main object is the ndarray (N-dimensional array), which is a versatile data structure for representing arrays of homogeneous data types. NumPy arrays offer several advantages over Python lists, including:

- More efficient storage and computation.
- Optimized operations for array manipulation.
- Broadcasting, which allows for element-wise operations on arrays of different shapes.

```python
import numpy as np
# Example of creating a NumPy array from a Python list
arr = np.array([1, 2, 3, 4, 5])
print(arr)
# Output: [1 2 3 4 5]
```

3. Array Creation:

NumPy provides various functions for creating arrays with different shapes and initial values:

```python
# Example of creating a NumPy array with zeros
zeros_arr = np.zeros((3, 4)) # Create a 3x4 array filled with zeros
print(zeros_arr)
# Example of creating a NumPy array with ones
ones_arr = np.ones((2, 3)) # Create a 2x3 array filled with ones
print(ones_arr)
# Example of creating a NumPy array with a specified range of values
range_arr = np.arange(1, 10, 2) # Create an array with values from 1 to 9 (exclusive) with a step of 2
print(range_arr)
```

4. Array Operations:

NumPy provides a wide range of mathematical functions for operating on arrays, including element-wise operations, linear algebra, statistics, and more:

```python
# Example of performing element-wise operations on arrays
arr1 = np.array([1, 2, 3])
arr2 = np.array([4, 5, 6])
# Addition
```

```python
result_addition = arr1 + arr2
# Multiplication
result_multiplication = arr1 * arr2
print("Addition:", result_addition)
print("Multiplication:", result_multiplication)
# Output:
# Addition: [5 7 9]
# Multiplication: [ 4 10 18]
```

5. Indexing and Slicing:

You can access and manipulate elements of NumPy arrays using indexing and slicing, similar to Python lists:

```python
# Example of indexing and slicing NumPy arrays
arr = np.array([1, 2, 3, 4, 5])
# Accessing individual elements
print("Element at index 2:", arr[2])
# Slicing
print("Sliced array:", arr[1:4])
# Output:
# Element at index 2: 3
# Sliced array: [2 3 4]
```

6. Universal Functions (ufuncs):

NumPy provides universal functions (ufuncs) for element-wise operations on arrays, such as trigonometric functions, exponential functions, logarithms, and more:

```python
# Example of using universal functions (ufuncs)
arr = np.array([0, np.pi/2, np.pi])
# Sine function
sin_arr = np.sin(arr)
print("Sine:", sin_arr)
# Exponential function
exp_arr = np.exp(arr)
print("Exponential:", exp_arr)
# Output:
# Sine: [0.0000000e+00 1.0000000e+00 1.2246468e-16]
```

Exponential: [1. 4.81047738 23.14069263]

By leveraging NumPy in data handling and manipulation tasks, you can efficiently perform numerical computations, manipulate arrays, and implement complex mathematical operations, making it an indispensable tool for scientific computing and data analysis in Python.

Manipulating Data with Pandas:

Pandas is a powerful library in Python for data manipulation and analysis. It provides high-level data structures, such as Series and DataFrame, along with a wide range of functions for manipulating, cleaning, and analyzing structured data. In data handling and manipulation tasks, Pandas offers intuitive tools for importing, transforming, and analyzing data efficiently. Let's delve into Pandas in detail, along with examples to illustrate its usage:

1. **Installation:**

   Before using Pandas, you need to install it. You can install Pandas using pip, Python's package manager:

   pip install pandas

2. **Introduction to Pandas Data Structures:**

Pandas introduces two primary data structures: Series and DataFrame.

- **Series:** A one-dimensional array-like object containing a sequence of values and an associated array of labels called the index. It can hold any data type.

```
import pandas as pd
# Example of creating a Series
s = pd.Series([1, 2, 3, 4, 5])
print(s)
```

DataFrame: A two-dimensional labeled data structure with columns of potentially different data types. It is similar to a spreadsheet or SQL table, and it can be thought of as a dictionary of Series objects.

```python
# Example of creating a DataFrame from a dictionary
data = {'Name': ['Alice', 'Bob', 'Charlie', 'David'],
'Age': [25, 30, 35, 40]}
df = pd.DataFrame(data)
print(df)
```

3. Importing and Exporting Data:

Pandas provides functions for reading data from various file formats, such as CSV, Excel, SQL databases, and more.

```python
# Example of reading data from a CSV file
df = pd.read_csv('data.csv')
# Example of writing data to a CSV file
df.to_csv('output.csv', index=False)
```

4. Data Exploration and Manipulation:

Pandas offers powerful functions for exploring and manipulating data, including selecting, filtering, sorting, grouping, and aggregating data.

```python
# Example of selecting columns and rows
# Selecting a single column
print(df['Name'])
# Selecting multiple columns
print(df[['Name', 'Age']])
# Selecting rows based on a condition
print(df[df['Age'] > 30])
```

5. Data Cleaning:

Pandas simplifies the process of cleaning and preprocessing data by providing functions for handling missing values, duplicates, and outliers.

```python
# Example of handling missing values
# Drop rows with missing values
df.dropna()
```

```
# Fill missing values with a specific value
df.fillna(0)
# Example of handling duplicates
# Drop duplicate rows
df.drop_duplicates()
# Example of handling outliers
# Remove outliers based on a condition
df = df[(df['Age'] >= 20) & (df['Age'] <= 60)]
```

6. Data Aggregation and Grouping:

Pandas enables you to aggregate and summarize data by grouping it based on one or more variables.

```
# Example of grouping data and calculating aggregate statistics
# Grouping by a column and calculating mean age
grouped_df = df.groupby('Name').mean()
print(grouped_df)
```

7. Data Visualization:

Pandas integrates with Matplotlib and other visualization libraries to facilitate data visualization.

```
# Example of plotting data
import matplotlib.pyplot as plt
# Plotting a histogram of ages
df['Age'].plot(kind='hist', bins=10)
plt.xlabel('Age')
plt.ylabel('Frequency')
plt.title('Distribution of Ages')
plt.show()
```

By leveraging Pandas in data handling and manipulation tasks, you can efficiently import, clean, transform, and analyze structured data, enabling you to derive insights and make data-driven decisions effectively.

Chapter 4: Introduction to AI Libraries

AI libraries provide a rich set of tools and algorithms for building and deploying artificial intelligence applications. These libraries offer functionalities ranging from basic machine learning algorithms to advanced deep learning models, making them indispensable for AI practitioners. Let's explore some popular AI libraries in detail, along with examples to illustrate their usage:

Overview Of Popular AI Libraries in Python:

1. **TensorFlow:**

   TensorFlow is an open-source machine learning framework developed by Google. It provides a comprehensive ecosystem for building and deploying machine learning models, including deep neural networks.

```python
import tensorflow as tf
# Example of creating a simple neural network model using TensorFlow
model = tf.keras.Sequential([
tf.keras.layers.Dense(64, activation='relu', input_shape=(784,)),
tf.keras.layers.Dense(10, activation='softmax')
])
```

2. **PyTorch:**

PyTorch is an open-source machine learning library developed by Facebook's AI Research lab. It is known for its dynamic computation graph and ease of use, making it popular among researchers and practitioners.

```python
import torch
import torch.nn as nn
# Example of creating a simple neural network model using PyTorch
class SimpleNN(nn.Module):
def __init__(self):
super(SimpleNN, self).__init__()
self.fc1 = nn.Linear(784, 64)
self.fc2 = nn.Linear(64, 10)
def forward(self, x):
x = torch.relu(self.fc1(x))
x = torch.softmax(self.fc2(x), dim=1)
return x
model = SimpleNN()
```

3. **Scikit-learn:**

Scikit-learn is a versatile machine learning library in Python that provides simple and efficient tools for data mining and data analysis. It includes various algorithms for classification, regression, clustering, dimensionality reduction, and more.

```python
from sklearn.datasets import load_iris
from sklearn.model_selection import train_test_split
from sklearn.ensemble import RandomForestClassifier
from sklearn.metrics import accuracy_score
# Example of using Scikit-learn for classification
iris = load_iris()
X_train, X_test, y_train, y_test = train_test_split(iris.data, iris.target, test_size=0.2, random_state=42)
clf = RandomForestClassifier()
clf.fit(X_train, y_train)
```

```python
y_pred = clf.predict(X_test)
accuracy = accuracy_score(y_test, y_pred)
print("Accuracy:", accuracy)
```

4. **Keras:**

Keras is a high-level neural networks API written in Python and capable of running on top of TensorFlow, Theano, or Microsoft Cognitive Toolkit (CNTK). It is designed for rapid prototyping and experimentation with deep learning models.

```python
from keras.models import Sequential
from keras.layers import Dense
# Example of creating a simple neural network model using Keras
model = Sequential([
Dense(64, activation='relu', input_shape=(784,)),
Dense(10, activation='softmax')
])
```

5. **OpenAI Gym:**

OpenAI Gym is a toolkit for developing and comparing reinforcement learning algorithms. It provides a collection of environments (e.g., classic control, Atari games) to test and benchmark reinforcement learning algorithms.

```python
import gym
# Example of using OpenAI Gym environment
env = gym.make('CartPole-v1')
observation = env.reset()
for _ in range(1000):
env.render()
action = env.action_space.sample() # Random action
observation, reward, done, info = env.step(action)
if done:
break
env.close()
```

By leveraging these AI libraries, developers and researchers can build, train, and deploy a wide range of artificial intelligence applications, from simple machine learning models to complex deep learning networks and reinforcement learning agents. Each library offers unique features and capabilities, catering to different needs and preferences in the AI community.

Installation And Setup of AI Libraries:

Before diving into the exciting world of artificial intelligence (AI) development, it's essential to properly install and set up the required AI libraries on your system. Here, we'll walk you through the process of installing some popular AI libraries in Python, including TensorFlow, Keras, and PyTorch, along with examples to help you get started:

1. **TensorFlow:**

   TensorFlow can be installed via pip, Python's package manager. If you have a GPU-enabled system and want to leverage GPU acceleration, you can install the GPU version of TensorFlow, which requires additional dependencies like CUDA and cuDNN.

   # CPU version

   pip install tensorflow

   # GPU version

   pip install tensorflow-gpu

2. **Keras:**

   Keras is a high-level neural networks API that works seamlessly with TensorFlow, Theano, and Microsoft Cognitive Toolkit (CNTK). Since Keras is included as part of TensorFlow 2.0 and later versions, you don't need to install it separately when using TensorFlow.

   # Keras is included in TensorFlow 2.0 and later versions

   pip install tensorflow

3. **PyTorch:**

PyTorch can also be installed via pip. You can choose between CPU-only or GPU-enabled versions based on your system configuration.

```
# CPU version
pip install torch torchvision torchaudio
# GPU version (requires CUDA and cuDNN)
pip install torch torchvision torchaudio torch.cuda
```

4. **Example:**

Let's verify the installation of TensorFlow by writing a simple Python script to create and train a neural network model:

```
import tensorflow as tf
from tensorflow.keras.models import Sequential
from tensorflow.keras.layers import Dense
# Create a simple neural network model
model = Sequential([
Dense(64, activation='relu', input_shape=(784,)),
Dense(10, activation='softmax')
])
# Compile the model
model.compile(optimizer='adam',
loss='sparse_categorical_crossentropy',
metrics=['accuracy'])
# Train the model (dummy data used for illustration)
model.fit(x_train, y_train, epochs=5, batch_size=32)
```

By following these installation steps and running the example code, you'll have TensorFlow up and running on your system, ready to embark on your AI journey.

Installing and setting up AI libraries is the first step towards building powerful AI applications. By following the installation instructions provided for TensorFlow, Keras, PyTorch, and other AI libraries, you'll be well-equipped to start exploring and experimenting with AI algorithms and models. Remember to check the official documentation for each library for any additional installation instructions or system requirements specific to your environment.

Introduction to Neural Networks:

Neural networks are a fundamental component of artificial intelligence (AI) and machine learning. They are inspired by the structure and function of the human brain, consisting of interconnected layers of artificial neurons that process input data and produce output predictions. Here, we'll provide an overview of neural networks, including their architecture, key components, and examples to illustrate their functionality:

1. **Neural Network Architecture:**

   Neural networks are organized into layers, with each layer comprising multiple neurons (also called nodes or units). The basic architecture of a neural network typically includes three types of layers:

   Input Layer: This layer receives input data and passes it to the subsequent layers for processing. The number of neurons in the input layer corresponds to the number of features in the input data.

   Hidden Layers: These intermediate layers perform complex transformations on the input data through weighted connections between neurons. Hidden layers enable neural networks to learn intricate patterns and relationships within the data.

   Output Layer: This layer produces the final output prediction based on the processed input data. The number of neurons in the output layer depends on the nature of the task (e.g., classification, regression).

2. **Key Components of Neural Networks:**

   Neurons: Neurons are the basic processing units of neural networks. Each neuron receives input signals, computes a weighted sum of the inputs, applies an activation function to the sum, and produces an output signal.

Weights: Weights represent the strength of connections between neurons in adjacent layers. They determine how input signals are combined and transformed as they pass through the network. Training a neural network involves adjusting the weights to minimize the prediction error.

Activation Functions: Activation functions introduce non-linearity into the network, enabling it to learn complex patterns and make non-linear predictions. Common activation functions include sigmoid, tanh, ReLU (Rectified Linear Unit), and softmax.

3. **Example:**

Let's consider a simple example of building a neural network for image classification using TensorFlow/Keras:

```
import tensorflow as tf
from tensorflow.keras import layers, models
# Define the neural network architecture
model = models.Sequential([
layers.Flatten(input_shape=(28, 28)), # Input layer (flatten 28x28 images)
layers.Dense(128, activation='relu'), # Hidden layer with 128 neurons and ReLU activation
layers.Dense(10, activation='softmax') # Output layer with 10 neurons (for 10 classes) and softmax activation
])
# Compile the model
model.compile(optimizer='adam',
loss='sparse_categorical_crossentropy',
metrics=['accuracy'])
# Train the model on training data (x_train, y_train)
model.fit(x_train, y_train, epochs=10, batch_size=32)
```

```
# Evaluate the model on test data (x_test, y_test)
test_loss, test_accuracy = model.evaluate(x_test, y_test)
print("Test Accuracy:", test_accuracy)
```

In this example, we create a neural network with one hidden layer and one output layer using TensorFlow/Keras. We compile the model with an optimizer, loss function, and evaluation metrics, then train the model on training data and evaluate its performance on test data.

Conclusion:

Neural networks are powerful models capable of learning complex patterns and making accurate predictions across various domains, including image recognition, natural language processing, and reinforcement learning. By understanding the architecture and components of neural networks, you'll be equipped to design and train your own models to tackle real-world AI challenges.

Chapter 5: Building Neural Networks

TensorFlow and Keras are two of the most widely used libraries for building neural networks in Python. TensorFlow provides a flexible framework for defining and training deep learning models, while Keras offers a high-level API that simplifies the process of building and experimenting with neural networks. Here, we'll delve into the process of building neural networks using TensorFlow and Keras, including key concepts and examples to demonstrate their usage:

1. **Setting up the Environment:**

   Before building neural networks with TensorFlow and Keras, ensure that you have both libraries installed in your Python environment:

   pip install tensorflow

2. **Defining the Neural Network Architecture:**

   Neural networks are composed of layers, each performing specific computations on the input data. In TensorFlow/Keras, you can define the architecture of your neural network using the **Sequential** API or the functional API.

   import tensorflow as tf

   from tensorflow.keras import layers, models

   # Define a Sequential model

   model = models.Sequential([

```python
layers.Dense(64, activation='relu', input_shape=(784,)),
layers.Dense(10, activation='softmax')
])
# Alternatively, use the functional API
inputs = tf.keras.Input(shape=(784,))
x = layers.Dense(64, activation='relu')(inputs)
outputs = layers.Dense(10, activation='softmax')(x)
model = tf.keras.Model(inputs=inputs, outputs=outputs)
```

3. **Compiling the Model:**

   Once the model architecture is defined, you need to compile it with an optimizer, loss function, and optional evaluation metrics. This step prepares the model for training.

```python
model.compile(optimizer='adam',
loss='sparse_categorical_crossentropy',
metrics=['accuracy'])
```

4. **Training the Model:**

   After compiling the model, you can train it on training data using the **fit** method. Specify the number of epochs (iterations over the entire dataset) and the batch size (number of samples per gradient update).

```python
model.fit(x_train, y_train, epochs=10, batch_size=32)
```

5. **Evaluating the Model:**

   Once trained, evaluate the model's performance on test data using the **evaluate** method.

```python
test_loss, test_accuracy = model.evaluate(x_test, y_test)
print("Test Accuracy:", test_accuracy)
```

6. **Making Predictions:**

   After training, you can use the trained model to make predictions on new data using the **predict** method.

```python
predictions = model.predict(x_new_data)
```

7. **Example:**

Here's an example of building a simple neural network for image classification using TensorFlow and Keras:

```
import tensorflow as tf
from tensorflow.keras import layers, models
# Define the neural network architecture
model = models.Sequential([
layers.Flatten(input_shape=(28, 28)), # Input layer (flatten 28x28 images)
layers.Dense(128, activation='relu'), # Hidden layer with 128 neurons and ReLU activation
layers.Dense(10, activation='softmax') # Output layer with 10 neurons (for 10 classes) and softmax activation
])
# Compile the model
model.compile(optimizer='adam',
loss='sparse_categorical_crossentropy',
metrics=['accuracy'])
# Train the model on training data (x_train, y_train)
model.fit(x_train, y_train, epochs=10, batch_size=32)
# Evaluate the model on test data (x_test, y_test)
test_loss, test_accuracy = model.evaluate(x_test, y_test)
print("Test Accuracy:", test_accuracy)
```

Conclusion:

Building neural networks with TensorFlow and Keras enables you to create sophisticated models for various tasks, such as image classification, natural language processing, and reinforcement learning. By following the steps outlined above and experimenting with different architectures and hyperparameters, you can develop powerful AI models to solve real-world problems.

Understanding Neural Network Architecture:

Neural network architecture forms the backbone of deep learning models, defining the structure and connectivity between layers of artificial neurons. Understanding the architecture of neural networks is crucial for designing effective models to solve diverse AI tasks. Below, we'll delve into the components of neural network architecture and provide examples to illustrate their significance:

1. **Input Layer:**

The input layer is the initial layer of the neural network, responsible for receiving input data. Each neuron in the input layer represents a feature or dimension of the input data. The number of neurons in the input layer is determined by the dimensionality of the input data.

Example: In an image classification task, the input layer of a convolutional neural network (CNN) may consist of neurons corresponding to the pixels of an image.

The input layer is the gateway of information into a neural network. It receives the raw data or features and passes them to subsequent layers for processing. Understanding the input layer is crucial as it sets the foundation for how data is represented and processed throughout the network. Here's a comprehensive overview of the input layer in neural network architecture:

1. **Role of the Input Layer:**

- The input layer receives the raw input data or features.
- Each neuron in the input layer represents a feature or dimension of the input data.
- The number of neurons in the input layer corresponds to the dimensionality of the input data.

2. **Data Representation:**

- Input data can be in various forms such as images, text, time series, or numerical data.

- Input data is often preprocessed and normalized before being fed into the neural network.
- For images, each pixel value may be represented by a neuron in the input layer.
- For text data, words may be encoded into numerical vectors or one-hot encoded before being input to the network.
- For numerical data, each feature may be represented by a neuron in the input layer.

3. Example:

- Consider a simple example of building a neural network for image classification using TensorFlow and Keras:

```
import tensorflow as tf
from tensorflow.keras import layers, models
# Define the neural network architecture
model = models.Sequential([
layers.Flatten(input_shape=(28, 28)), # Input layer (flatten 28x28 images)
layers.Dense(128, activation='relu'), # Hidden layer with 128 neurons and ReLU activation
layers.Dense(10, activation='softmax') # Output layer with 10 neurons (for 10 classes) and softmax activation
])
```

In this example, the input layer consists of neurons that receive flattened 28x28 pixel images as input for image classification.

4. Importance of Input Layer:

- The input layer plays a critical role in shaping the neural network's architecture and defining how data is processed.
- Proper understanding and preprocessing of input data ensure that the neural network can effectively learn and generalize from the data.

- The input layer sets the stage for subsequent layers to extract relevant features and patterns from the input data.

II. Hidden Layers:

Hidden layers are intermediate layers between the input and output layers, where the bulk of computation and feature extraction occurs. Each neuron in a hidden layer receives input from neurons in the previous layer and produces an output based on weighted sums of these inputs.

Example: In a feedforward neural network, hidden layers apply linear transformations and non-linear activation functions to the input data to learn complex patterns and representations.

Hidden layers are an integral component of neural network architecture, responsible for processing input data and extracting meaningful features before producing output predictions. They contribute to the network's ability to learn complex patterns and relationships within the data. Here's a comprehensive overview of hidden layers in neural networks, along with examples to illustrate their significance:

1. **Role of Hidden Layers:**

- Hidden layers perform computations on the input data received from the input layer.
- They learn and extract hierarchical representations of the input data through weighted connections between neurons.
- Hidden layers enable neural networks to capture intricate patterns and relationships that may not be apparent in the raw input data.

2. **Activation Functions:**

- Neurons in hidden layers apply activation functions to introduce non-linearity into the network, allowing it to model complex mappings between inputs and outputs.
- Common activation functions used in hidden layers include Rectified Linear Unit (ReLU), sigmoid, tanh, and softmax.

3. Depth of Neural Networks:

- The depth of a neural network refers to the number of hidden layers it contains.
- Deeper networks with multiple hidden layers have a higher capacity to learn intricate patterns and representations from the data.
- However, increasing the depth of the network also introduces challenges such as vanishing or exploding gradients during training.

4. Example:

- Consider a feedforward neural network with multiple hidden layers for image classification using TensorFlow and Keras:

```
import tensorflow as tf
from tensorflow.keras import layers, models
# Define the neural network architecture with multiple hidden layers
model = models.Sequential([
layers.Flatten(input_shape=(28, 28)), # Input layer (flatten 28x28 images)
layers.Dense(128, activation='relu'), # First hidden layer with 128 neurons and ReLU activation
layers.Dense(64, activation='relu'), # Second hidden layer with 64 neurons and ReLU activation
layers.Dense(10, activation='softmax') # Output layer with 10 neurons (for 10 classes) and softmax activation
```

```
])
```

In this example, the neural network contains two hidden layers with ReLU activation functions, enabling the network to learn and extract hierarchical features from the flattened input images.

5. Importance of Hidden Layers:

- Hidden layers play a crucial role in enabling neural networks to learn and represent complex patterns and relationships within the data.
- They allow neural networks to generalize well to unseen data by capturing informative features from the input data.
- The depth and configuration of hidden layers significantly impact the performance and capacity of the neural network.

III. Output Layer:

The output layer is the final layer of the neural network, responsible for producing the model's predictions or outputs. The number of neurons in the output layer depends on the nature of the task (e.g., classification, regression). For classification tasks, each neuron typically represents a class label, while for regression tasks, there may be a single neuron representing the predicted value.

Example: In a binary classification task, the output layer of a neural network may consist of a single neuron with a sigmoid activation function, producing a probability score indicating the likelihood of the positive class.

The output layer is the final layer of a neural network, responsible for producing the network's predictions or outputs based on the processed input data. It plays a crucial role in determining the format and interpretation of the network's output, depending on the task at hand. Below is a comprehensive overview of the output layer in neural network architecture, along with examples to illustrate its significance:

1. Role of the Output Layer:

- The output layer transforms the processed input data into the desired format for the specific task.
- It typically contains one or more neurons, with each neuron representing a class label, a regression value, or a probability distribution over classes.
- The activation function used in the output layer depends on the nature of the task (e.g., classification, regression).

2. Activation Functions:

- The choice of activation function in the output layer depends on the type of problem being solved:
    - For binary classification tasks, the sigmoid or logistic activation function is commonly used to produce binary class probabilities.
    - For multi-class classification tasks, the softmax activation function is used to generate a probability distribution over multiple classes, ensuring that the output probabilities sum to one.
    - For regression tasks, no activation function or linear activation function is typically used to produce continuous output values.

3. Example:

- Consider examples of neural networks for different types of tasks using TensorFlow and Keras:

1. **Binary Classification:**

```
import tensorflow as tf
from tensorflow.keras import layers, models
# Define the neural network architecture for binary classification
model = models.Sequential([
```

```
layers.Dense(64, activation='relu', input_shape=(X_train.shape[1],)),
layers.Dense(1, activation='sigmoid') # Output layer with sigmoid activation for binary classification
])
```

2. **Multi-class Classification:**

```
import tensorflow as tf
from tensorflow.keras import layers, models
# Define the neural network architecture for multi-class classification
model = models.Sequential([
layers.Dense(64, activation='relu', input_shape=(X_train.shape[1],)),
layers.Dense(num_classes, activation='softmax') # Output layer with softmax activation for multi-class classification
])
```

3. **Regression:**

```
import tensorflow as tf
from tensorflow.keras import layers, models
# Define the neural network architecture for regression
model = models.Sequential([
layers.Dense(64, activation='relu', input_shape=(X_train.shape[1],)),
layers.Dense(1) # Output layer without activation for regression
])
```

4. **Importance of the Output Layer:**

- The output layer determines the format and interpretation of the network's predictions, making it crucial for achieving the desired task performance.

- Proper selection of activation functions and output formats ensures that the network outputs meaningful predictions for the given task.
- The output layer's design directly impacts the loss function used for training the network and the evaluation metrics used to assess its performance.

IV. Activation Functions:

Activation functions introduce non-linearity into the neural network, enabling it to learn complex mappings between inputs and outputs. Common activation functions include sigmoid, tanh, ReLU (Rectified Linear Unit), and softmax.

Example: ReLU is a widely used activation function in hidden layers due to its simplicity and effectiveness in mitigating the vanishing gradient problem.

Activation functions play a crucial role in neural network architecture by introducing non-linearity into the model, enabling it to learn complex patterns and relationships within the data. They determine the output of each neuron in a neural network, influencing the network's ability to approximate non-linear functions. Below is a comprehensive overview of activation functions in neural networks, along with examples to illustrate their significance:

1. **Role of Activation Functions:**

- Activation functions introduce non-linearity into the network, allowing it to model complex mappings between inputs and outputs.
- They squash the output of each neuron into a specific range, typically between 0 and 1 or -1 and 1, depending on the activation function used.
- Activation functions enable neural networks to learn and represent complex patterns and relationships within the data.

2. Common Activation Functions:

- **Sigmoid (Logistic):**
  - Formula: $\sigma(x) = 1 + e{-}x1$
  - Output Range: (0, 1)
  - Used in: Binary classification problems where the output needs to be interpreted as probabilities.

- **Hyperbolic Tangent (Tanh):**
  - Formula: $\tanh(x) = ex + e{-}xex{-}e{-}x$
  - Output Range: (-1, 1)
  - Used in: Hidden layers of neural networks, especially for standardizing inputs.

- **Rectified Linear Unit (ReLU):**
  - Formula: $\text{ReLU}(x) = \max(0, x)$
  - Output Range: (0, +∞)
  - Used in: Hidden layers of deep neural networks due to its simplicity and effectiveness in mitigating the vanishing gradient problem.

- **Leaky ReLU:**
  - Formula: Leaky $\text{ReLU}(x) = \max(\alpha x, x)$, where α is a small positive slope for negative inputs.
  - Output Range: (-∞, +∞)
  - Used in: Deep neural networks to address the dying ReLU problem by allowing small negative gradients for negative inputs.

- **Softmax:**
  - Formula: $\text{softmax}(xi) = \Sigma jNexjexi$ for each output neuron xi
  - Output Range: (0, 1) and sum to 1 across all output neurons.
  - Used in: Multi-class classification problems where the output needs to be interpreted as class probabilities.

3. Example:

- Implementation of different activation functions in a neural network using TensorFlow and Keras:

```python
import tensorflow as tf
from tensorflow.keras import layers, models
# Define the neural network architecture with different activation functions
model = models.Sequential([
layers.Dense(64, activation='sigmoid', input_shape=(X_train.shape[1],)), # Sigmoid activation function
layers.Dense(64, activation='tanh'), # Tanh activation function
layers.Dense(64, activation='relu'), # ReLU activation function
layers.Dense(64, activation=tf.keras.layers.LeakyReLU(alpha=0.1)), # Leaky ReLU activation function
layers.Dense(num_classes, activation='softmax') # Softmax activation function
])
```

4. Importance of Activation Functions:

- Activation functions enable neural networks to model complex relationships and non-linear mappings between inputs and outputs.
- Proper selection of activation functions is crucial for achieving optimal performance and preventing issues such as vanishing or exploding gradients during training.
- Different activation functions are suitable for different tasks and architectures, and experimentation is necessary to find the most appropriate activation functions for a given problem.

V. Connectivity Patterns:

Neural networks exhibit various connectivity patterns between layers, including fully connected (dense) layers, convolutional layers, recurrent layers, and skip connections (residual connections). Each connectivity pattern influences the model's capacity to learn and represent complex relationships in the data.

Example: Convolutional neural networks (CNNs) leverage shared weights and local connectivity to capture spatial patterns in images efficiently, making them well-suited for tasks such as image classification and object detection.

Connectivity patterns in neural network architecture define how neurons in different layers are interconnected, influencing the flow of information through the network and the network's ability to learn and represent complex relationships within the data. Different connectivity patterns, such as fully connected (dense) layers, convolutional layers, recurrent layers, and skip connections (residual connections), have distinct properties and are suited for different types of tasks. Below is a comprehensive overview of connectivity patterns in neural networks, along with examples to illustrate their significance:

1. **Fully Connected (Dense) Layers:**

   - **Description:** In fully connected layers, also known as dense layers, each neuron in a layer is connected to every neuron in the preceding layer.
   - **Usage:** Fully connected layers are commonly used in feedforward neural networks for tasks such as classification and regression.
   - **Example:** Consider a simple feedforward neural network with fully connected layers using TensorFlow and Keras:

```
import tensorflow as tf
from tensorflow.keras import layers, models
# Define the neural network architecture with fully connected
(dense) layers
```

```
model = models.Sequential([
layers.Flatten(input_shape=(28, 28)), # Input layer (flatten 28x28 images)
layers.Dense(128, activation='relu'), # Fully connected hidden layer with 128 neurons
layers.Dense(10, activation='softmax') # Output layer with 10 neurons for classification
])
```

2. Convolutional Layers:

- **Description:** Convolutional layers apply convolution operations to input data, enabling the network to learn spatial hierarchies of features.
- **Usage:** Convolutional layers are commonly used in convolutional neural networks (CNNs) for tasks such as image classification, object detection, and image segmentation.
- **Example:** Consider a simple CNN architecture with convolutional and pooling layers using TensorFlow and Keras:

```
import tensorflow as tf
from tensorflow.keras import layers, models
# Define the convolutional neural network architecture
model = models.Sequential([
layers.Conv2D(32, (3, 3), activation='relu', input_shape=(28, 28, 1)), # Convolutional layer with 32 filters
layers.MaxPooling2D((2, 2)), # Max pooling layer
layers.Conv2D(64, (3, 3), activation='relu'), # Convolutional layer with 64 filters
layers.MaxPooling2D((2, 2)), # Max pooling layer
layers.Flatten(), # Flatten layer
layers.Dense(64, activation='relu'), # Fully connected hidden layer
layers.Dense(10, activation='softmax') # Output layer
])
```

3. Recurrent Layers:

- **Description:** Recurrent layers enable neural networks to model sequential data by maintaining internal state (memory) and processing sequences iteratively.
- **Usage:** Recurrent layers are commonly used in recurrent neural networks (RNNs) for tasks such as time series prediction, natural language processing, and sequence generation.
- **Example:** Consider a simple RNN architecture for sequence prediction using TensorFlow and Keras:

```python
import tensorflow as tf
from tensorflow.keras import layers, models
# Define the recurrent neural network architecture
model = models.Sequential([
layers.SimpleRNN(32, input_shape=(None, 28)), # Recurrent layer with 32 units
layers.Dense(10, activation='softmax') # Output layer
])
```

4. Skip Connections (Residual Connections):

- **Description:** Skip connections allow the direct flow of information between layers, bypassing one or more intermediate layers.
- **Usage:** Skip connections are commonly used in deep neural networks to alleviate the vanishing gradient problem and facilitate training of very deep networks.
- **Example:** Consider a residual block with skip connections in a deep neural network using TensorFlow and Keras:

```python
import tensorflow as tf
from tensorflow.keras import layers, models
# Define a residual block with skip connections
def residual_block(x, filters):
```

```
    y = layers.Conv2D(filters, (3, 3), padding='same', activation='relu')(x)
    y = layers.Conv2D(filters, (3, 3), padding='same', activation='relu')(y)
    return layers.add([x, y])
    # Define the deep neural network architecture with residual connections
    inputs = layers.Input(shape=(28, 28, 1))
    x = layers.Conv2D(32, (3, 3), activation='relu')(inputs)
    x = residual_block(x, 32)
    x = layers.MaxPooling2D((2, 2))(x)
    x = layers.Conv2D(64, (3, 3), activation='relu')(x)
    x = residual_block(x, 64)
    x = layers.MaxPooling2D((2, 2))(x)
    x = layers.Flatten()(x)
    x = layers.Dense(64, activation='relu')(x)
    outputs = layers.Dense(10, activation='softmax')(x)
    model = models.Model(inputs, outputs)
```

Understanding the architecture of neural networks is essential for designing effective models tailored to specific AI tasks. By grasping the roles and functionalities of input layers, hidden layers, output layers, activation functions, and connectivity patterns, you can develop neural networks capable of learning intricate patterns and making accurate predictions across diverse domains. Experimenting with different architectures and configurations enables you to optimize model performance and tackle complex AI challenges effectively.

Building And Training Neural Networks:

Building and training neural networks using TensorFlow and Keras involves a series of steps, from defining the network architecture to optimizing its performance through training. TensorFlow provides a flexible framework for building and deploying deep learning models, while Keras offers a high-level API for designing and training neural networks with ease. Below is a comprehensive guide on building and training neural networks using TensorFlow and Keras, accompanied by examples to illustrate each step:

1. **Defining the Neural Network Architecture:**

- Begin by defining the architecture of the neural network, including the number of layers, types of layers, and activation functions.
- Use the **Sequential** API in Keras to create a sequential model, or the functional API for more complex architectures.
- Specify the input shape for the first layer based on the dimensions of the input data.

Example:

```
import tensorflow as tf
from tensorflow.keras import layers, models
# Define a sequential model
model = models.Sequential([
layers.Dense(64, activation='relu', input_shape=(input_shape,)),
layers.Dense(32, activation='relu'),
layers.Dense(num_classes, activation='softmax')
])
```

2. **Compiling the Model:**

- After defining the architecture, compile the model with appropriate loss function, optimizer, and evaluation metrics.
- Specify the loss function based on the task (e.g., categorical cross-entropy for classification, mean squared error for regression).
- Choose an optimizer (e.g., Adam, SGD) to update the network's weights during training.
- Specify evaluation metrics to monitor during training (e.g., accuracy for classification).

Example:

```
model.compile(optimizer='adam',
loss='sparse_categorical_crossentropy',
metrics=['accuracy'])
```

3. Training the Model:

- Train the model on training data using the **fit** method.
- Specify the number of epochs (iterations over the entire dataset) and the batch size (number of samples per gradient update).
- Provide the training data (input features and corresponding labels) to the **fit** method.

Example:

```
model.fit(x_train, y_train, epochs=10, batch_size=32)
```

4. Evaluating the Model:

- Evaluate the trained model on test data to assess its performance.
- Use the **evaluate** method to compute the loss and evaluation metrics on the test data.

Example:

```
test_loss, test_accuracy = model.evaluate(x_test, y_test)
print("Test Loss:", test_loss)
print("Test Accuracy:", test_accuracy)
```

5. Making Predictions:

- Once trained, use the trained model to make predictions on new data.
- Use the **predict** method to generate predictions for input data.

Example:

```
predictions = model.predict(x_new_data)
```

6. Fine-tuning and Hyperparameter Tuning:

- Experiment with different architectures, activation functions, optimizers, and hyperparameters to optimize model performance.
- Use techniques such as cross-validation and grid search to find the best hyperparameters for the model.

Example:

```python
from sklearn.model_selection import GridSearchCV
from tensorflow.keras.wrappers.scikit_learn import KerasClassifier
# Define a function to create the model
def create_model(optimizer='adam', activation='relu'):
model = models.Sequential([
layers.Dense(64, activation=activation, input_shape=(input_shape,)),
layers.Dense(32, activation=activation),
layers.Dense(num_classes, activation='softmax')
])
model.compile(optimizer=optimizer,
loss='sparse_categorical_crossentropy',
metrics=['accuracy'])
return model
# Create a KerasClassifier with the create_model function
model = KerasClassifier(build_fn=create_model)
# Define hyperparameters to search
param_grid = {'batch_size': [32, 64],
'epochs': [10, 20],
'optimizer': ['adam', 'sgd'],
'activation': ['relu', 'tanh']}
# Perform grid search to find the best hyperparameters
grid = GridSearchCV(estimator=model, param_grid=param_grid, cv=3)
grid_result = grid.fit(x_train, y_train)
```

Print the best hyperparameters

print("Best: %f using %s" % (grid_result.best_score_, grid_result.best_params_))

7. Saving and Loading Models:

- Save the trained model to disk for future use or deployment.
- Use the **save** and **load_model** functions in TensorFlow/Keras to save and load models.

Example:

Save the trained model to disk

model.save('my_model.h5')

Load the saved model

loaded_model = models.load_model('my_model.h5')

Building and training neural networks using TensorFlow and Keras is a fundamental process in deep learning. By following the steps outlined above and experimenting with different architectures and hyperparameters, developers can create powerful models capable of solving a wide range of tasks, from image classification to natural language processing. Continuous iteration and optimization are key to achieving optimal performance in neural network models.

Implementing Basic Deep Learning Models:

In the realm of deep learning, understanding fundamental architectures like the perceptron and feedforward neural networks is essential. These models serve as building blocks for more complex networks and provide insights into how neural networks operate. Here's a comprehensive guide on implementing these basic deep learning models using TensorFlow and Keras, accompanied by examples:

1. **Perceptron:**

- The perceptron is the simplest form of a neural network, consisting of a single layer of neurons with binary outputs. It's commonly used for binary classification tasks.

Implementation with TensorFlow and Keras:

```
import numpy as np
import tensorflow as tf
from tensorflow.keras.models import Sequential
from tensorflow.keras.layers import Dense
# Define the perceptron model
model = Sequential([
Dense(1, input_dim=2, activation='sigmoid') # Single neuron with sigmoid activation
])
# Compile the model
model.compile(optimizer='adam', loss='binary_crossentropy', metrics=['accuracy'])
# Define training data
X_train = np.array([[0, 0], [0, 1], [1, 0], [1, 1]])
y_train = np.array([0, 0, 0, 1])
# Train the model
model.fit(X_train, y_train, epochs=100, verbose=1)
```

2. Feedforward Neural Networks (FNN):

- Feedforward neural networks consist of multiple layers of neurons, including input, hidden, and output layers. They can handle more complex tasks by learning hierarchical representations of the data.

Implementation with TensorFlow and Keras:

```
import numpy as np
import tensorflow as tf
from tensorflow.keras.models import Sequential
```

```python
from tensorflow.keras.layers import Dense
# Define the feedforward neural network model
model = Sequential([
Dense(64, input_dim=2, activation='relu'), # Input layer with 64
neurons and ReLU activation
Dense(32, activation='relu'), # Hidden layer with 32 neurons and
ReLU activation
Dense(1, activation='sigmoid') # Output layer with 1 neuron and
sigmoid activation
])
# Compile the model
model.compile(optimizer='adam', loss='binary_crossentropy', metrics=['accuracy'])
# Define training data
X_train = np.array([[0, 0], [0, 1], [1, 0], [1, 1]])
y_train = np.array([0, 1, 1, 0])
# Train the model
model.fit(X_train, y_train, epochs=100, verbose=1)
```

Key Points:

- Both the perceptron and feedforward neural networks can be implemented using TensorFlow and Keras.
- Perceptrons are suitable for simple binary classification tasks with linear decision boundaries.
- Feedforward neural networks are more versatile and can handle complex tasks by learning hierarchical representations of the data.
- Activation functions like sigmoid and ReLU are commonly used in both perceptrons and feedforward neural networks to introduce non-linearity.
- Training these models involves specifying the optimizer, loss function, and training data, followed by fitting the model to the data through epochs.

Conclusion:

Implementing basic deep learning models like the perceptron and feedforward neural networks provides a solid foundation for understanding more complex architectures. By leveraging TensorFlow and Keras, developers can easily build, train, and experiment with these models to solve various machine learning tasks. As deep learning continues to evolve, mastering these fundamental concepts remains essential for advancing in the field.

Chapter 6: Advanced Deep Learning Techniques

Advanced deep learning techniques represent a step forward from traditional neural network architectures, offering more sophisticated methods for modeling complex data and improving model performance. These techniques leverage concepts such as regularization, optimization algorithms, advanced activation functions, and model ensembling to enhance the capabilities of deep learning models. Here's a comprehensive overview of some advanced deep learning techniques, along with examples to illustrate their applications:

1. **Regularization Techniques:**

- Regularization methods are used to prevent overfitting and improve the generalization performance of deep learning models.
- Examples of regularization techniques include L1 and L2 regularization, dropout, and batch normalization.

Example:

```python
from tensorflow.keras.models import Sequential
from tensorflow.keras.layers import Dense, Dropout
from tensorflow.keras import regularizers
model = Sequential([
Dense(64, activation='relu', input_dim=100),
```

```
Dropout(0.5),
Dense(32,        activation='relu',        kernel_regularizer=regulariz-
ers.l2(0.01)),
Dense(1, activation='sigmoid')
])
```

2. Optimization Algorithms:

- Optimization algorithms are used to update the parameters of neural networks during training, aiming to minimize the loss function.
- Examples of optimization algorithms include SGD (Stochastic Gradient Descent), Adam, RMSprop, and AdaGrad.

Example:

```
model.compile(optimizer='adam', loss='binary_crossentropy', met-
rics=['accuracy'])
```

3. Advanced Activation Functions:

- Advanced activation functions introduce non-linearities into neural networks, enabling them to learn complex patterns.
- Examples include Leaky ReLU, PReLU (Parametric ReLU), ELU (Exponential Linear Unit), and Swish.

Example:

```
from tensorflow.keras.layers import LeakyReLU
model.add(Dense(64, activation=LeakyReLU(alpha=0.1)))
```

4. Transfer Learning:

- Transfer learning involves leveraging pre-trained deep learning models and fine-tuning them for specific tasks.
- By using pre-trained models, developers can benefit from the knowledge learned on large datasets and apply it to smaller datasets with similar characteristics.

Example:

from tensorflow.keras.applications import VGG16
base_model = VGG16(weights='imagenet', include_top=False, input_shape=(224, 224, 3))

5. Model Ensembling:

- Model ensembling combines predictions from multiple models to improve overall performance.
- Techniques such as bagging, boosting, and stacking are commonly used for model ensembling.

Example:

from sklearn.ensemble import VotingClassifier
model1 = RandomForestClassifier()
model2 = GradientBoostingClassifier()
model3 = SVC()
ensemble_model = VotingClassifier(estimators=[('rf', model1), ('gb', model2), ('svc', model3)], voting='hard')
ensemble_model.fit(X_train, y_train)

6. Generative Adversarial Networks (GANs):

- GANs consist of two neural networks, a generator and a discriminator, which are trained simultaneously to generate realistic data samples.
- GANs have applications in image generation, data augmentation, and generating synthetic data.

Example:

from tensorflow.keras.models import Sequential
from tensorflow.keras.layers import Dense, Reshape, Flatten
from tensorflow.keras.layers import Conv2D, Conv2DTranspose
from tensorflow.keras.optimizers import Adam
generator = Sequential([

```
Dense(7*7*256, input_dim=noise_dim),
Reshape((7, 7, 256)),
Conv2DTranspose(128, (3,3), strides=(2,2), padding='same', activation='relu'),
Conv2DTranspose(64, (3,3), strides=(2,2), padding='same', activation='relu'),
Conv2DTranspose(1, (3,3), strides=(1,1), padding='same', activation='sigmoid')
])
```

Conclusion:

Advanced deep learning techniques offer a wide range of tools and methodologies to tackle complex tasks in machine learning and artificial intelligence. By understanding and implementing these techniques, developers can build more powerful and robust deep learning models capable of solving real-world problems across various domains. Experimentation and exploration of these techniques are essential for staying at the forefront of deep learning research and applications.

Convolutional Neural Networks (CNNs):

Convolutional Neural Networks (CNNs) represent a powerful class of deep learning models designed specifically for processing structured grid-like data, such as images and videos. They have revolutionized computer vision tasks by automatically learning hierarchical representations of visual data, enabling tasks like image classification, object detection, and semantic segmentation. Below is a comprehensive overview of CNNs, including their architecture, key components, and examples:

1. **Architecture of CNNs:**

- CNNs consist of multiple layers, including convolutional layers, pooling layers, and fully connected layers.

- Convolutional layers perform feature extraction by applying filters (kernels) to input images, capturing spatial patterns.
- Pooling layers reduce the spatial dimensions of the feature maps, preserving important information while reducing computational complexity.
- Fully connected layers perform classification or regression based on the learned features.

2. Key Components of CNNs:

Convolutional Layers: Convolutional layers apply convolutional operations to input images, extracting local features through sliding window operations. Each convolutional layer consists of multiple filters that learn specific features, such as edges, textures, or object parts.

Pooling Layers: Pooling layers downsample feature maps, reducing spatial dimensions while preserving important information. Common pooling operations include max pooling and average pooling.

Activation Functions: Activation functions introduce non-linearity into the network, enabling CNNs to learn complex mappings between input and output. Common activation functions include ReLU (Rectified Linear Unit), Leaky ReLU, and PReLU.

Normalization Layers: Normalization layers like Batch Normalization can improve the stability and speed of CNN training by normalizing the activations of each layer.

Dropout: Dropout is a regularization technique used to prevent overfitting by randomly dropping a fraction of neurons during training, forcing the network to learn more robust features.

Padding: Padding is applied to input images to ensure that the spatial dimensions of feature maps remain consistent throughout the network. Zero-padding is commonly used to preserve spatial information at the borders.

Striding: Striding controls the step size of the sliding window during convolutional operations, affecting the spatial dimensions of feature maps. Larger strides result in smaller feature maps.

3. Example of CNN Architecture:

```python
from tensorflow.keras.models import Sequential
from tensorflow.keras.layers import Conv2D, MaxPooling2D, Flatten, Dense
model = Sequential([
Conv2D(32, (3, 3), activation='relu', input_shape=(28, 28, 1)),
MaxPooling2D((2, 2)),
Conv2D(64, (3, 3), activation='relu'),
MaxPooling2D((2, 2)),
Conv2D(64, (3, 3), activation='relu'),
Flatten(),
Dense(64, activation='relu'),
Dense(10, activation='softmax')
])
```

4. Applications of CNNs:

- Image Classification: CNNs can classify images into predefined categories, such as identifying objects in photographs.
- Object Detection: CNN-based object detection models can localize and classify objects within images, enabling applications like autonomous driving and surveillance.
- Semantic Segmentation: CNNs can segment images into meaningful regions, assigning each pixel a label corresponding to its semantic category.
- Image Generation: CNNs can generate new images by learning the underlying distribution of training data and sampling from it.

5. Pre-trained CNN Models:

- Pre-trained CNN models, such as VGG, ResNet, and MobileNet, have been trained on large-scale image datasets like ImageNet.
- These models can be fine-tuned on specific tasks or used as feature extractors for transfer learning.

Example:

from tensorflow.keras.applications import VGG16

base_model = VGG16(weights='imagenet', include_top=False, input_shape=(224, 224, 3))

Convolutional Neural Networks (CNNs) have become indispensable tools in the field of computer vision, enabling a wide range of applications from image classification to object detection and image generation. Understanding the architecture and components of CNNs, along with their applications and examples, is essential for effectively utilizing them in real-world scenarios. Continual research and innovation in CNNs continue to push the boundaries of what is possible in computer vision tasks.

Recurrent Neural Networks (RNNs):

Recurrent Neural Networks (RNNs) are a class of neural networks particularly suited for processing sequential data, making them well-suited for tasks such as time series prediction, natural language processing, and speech recognition. RNNs are designed to handle inputs of varying lengths and capture temporal dependencies within sequences. Below is a comprehensive overview of RNNs, including their architecture, key components, and examples:

1. **Architecture of RNNs:**

- RNNs consist of recurrent connections that allow information to persist over time, making them suitable for modeling sequential data.
- At each time step, the RNN processes an input vector and updates its hidden state based on the current input and the previous hidden state.
- The hidden state contains information about the sequence seen so far and is used to make predictions or generate outputs.

2. Key Components of RNNs:

Recurrent Connections: Recurrent connections enable information to flow from one time step to the next, allowing RNNs to capture temporal dependencies within sequences.

Hidden State: The hidden state of an RNN encodes information about the sequence seen so far and is updated at each time step.

Activation Function: Activation functions introduce non-linearity into the network, enabling RNNs to learn complex mappings between inputs and outputs. Common activation functions include tanh, ReLU, and sigmoid.

Sequence Length Handling: RNNs can handle inputs of variable lengths, making them suitable for tasks where sequence lengths vary.

3. Example of RNN Architecture:

```
from tensorflow.keras.models import Sequential
from tensorflow.keras.layers import SimpleRNN, Dense
model = Sequential([
SimpleRNN(64, input_shape=(T, D)),
Dense(10, activation='softmax')
])
```

4. Applications of RNNs:

- **Time Series Prediction:** RNNs can predict future values in time series data by learning patterns and trends from historical observations.

- **Natural Language Processing (NLP):** RNNs are widely used for tasks such as language modeling, text generation, sentiment analysis, and machine translation.

- **Speech Recognition:** RNNs can process audio waveforms and transcribe spoken language into text.

- **Sequence Generation:** RNNs can generate sequences of data, such as music, text, or images, by learning patterns from training data.

5. Example of NLP Application with RNNs:

```python
from tensorflow.keras.layers import Embedding, LSTM
model = Sequential([
Embedding(input_dim=vocab_size, output_dim=embedding_dim, input_length=max_seq_length),
LSTM(64),
Dense(num_classes, activation='softmax')
])
```

6. Long Short-Term Memory (LSTM) and Gated Recurrent Units (GRUs):

- LSTM and GRU are specialized variants of RNNs designed to address the vanishing gradient problem and capture long-range dependencies.
- LSTM and GRU introduce gating mechanisms to regulate the flow of information within the network, enabling better memory retention and learning of sequential patterns.

Example:

```python
from tensorflow.keras.layers import LSTM
model = Sequential([
LSTM(64, input_shape=(T, D)),
Dense(10, activation='softmax')
])
```

Recurrent Neural Networks (RNNs) are powerful tools for sequence modeling, capable of capturing temporal dependencies and patterns within sequential data. Understanding the architecture, components, and applications of RNNs is essential for effectively utilizing them in tasks such as time series prediction, natural language processing, and speech recognition. Continual research and innovation in RNNs continue to drive advancements in various domains, making them a foundational technique in deep learning.

Transfer Learning:

Transfer learning is a technique in deep learning where knowledge learned from solving one problem is applied to a different but related problem. It involves leveraging pre-trained models that have been trained on large datasets and fine-tuning them on a specific task or domain. This approach can significantly reduce the computational cost and training time required to achieve good performance on new tasks. Below is a comprehensive overview of transfer learning and fine-tuning pre-trained models, including their principles, methodologies, and examples:

1. **Principles of Transfer Learning:**

- Transfer learning exploits the idea that knowledge gained from solving one task can be beneficial for solving a related task.
- In deep learning, transfer learning involves reusing the learned feature representations of a pre-trained model for a new task.
- Pre-trained models are typically trained on large datasets (e.g., ImageNet for image classification) and have learned generic features that are transferable to other tasks.

2. **Methodologies of Transfer Learning:**

- **Feature Extraction:** In feature extraction, the pre-trained model is used as a fixed feature extractor, and only the top layers are replaced and retrained for the new task.
- **Fine-Tuning:** Fine-tuning involves unfreezing some or all of the layers of the pre-trained model and jointly training them with the new task's data, often with a lower learning rate.

3. **Example of Transfer Learning with Image Classification:**

```python
from tensorflow.keras.applications import MobileNetV2
```

```python
from tensorflow.keras.preprocessing.image import ImageDataGenerator
from tensorflow.keras.models import Sequential
from tensorflow.keras.layers import Dense, GlobalAveragePooling2D
# Load pre-trained MobileNetV2 model without top layers
base_model = MobileNetV2(weights='imagenet', include_top=False)
# Freeze the base model's layers
for layer in base_model.layers:
layer.trainable = False
# Add custom classification head
model = Sequential([
base_model,
GlobalAveragePooling2D(),
Dense(256, activation='relu'),
Dense(num_classes, activation='softmax')
])
# Compile the model
model.compile(optimizer='adam', loss='categorical_crossentropy', metrics=['accuracy'])
# Train the model with new data
model.fit(train_generator, validation_data=val_generator, epochs=10)
```

4. Example of Fine-Tuning with Text Classification:

```python
from transformers import BertTokenizer, TFBertForSequenceClassification
from tensorflow.keras.optimizers import Adam
# Load pre-trained BERT model
tokenizer = BertTokenizer.from_pretrained('bert-base-uncased')
bert_model = TFBertForSequenceClassification.from_pretrained('bert-base-uncased')
# Freeze all layers except classification head
for layer in bert_model.layers[:-1]:
```

```
layer.trainable = False
# Add custom classification head
model = Sequential([
bert_model,
Dense(num_classes, activation='softmax')
])
# Compile the model
optimizer = Adam(lr=1e-5)
model.compile(optimizer=optimizer,      loss='categorical_crossen-
tropy', metrics=['accuracy'])
# Train the model with new data
model.fit(train_dataset, validation_data=val_dataset, epochs=3)
```

5. Benefits of Transfer Learning and Fine-Tuning:

- **Reduced Training Time:** Transfer learning allows leveraging pre-trained models, reducing the computational cost and time required for training.
- **Improved Performance:** Pre-trained models have learned generic features from large datasets, which can lead to better performance on new tasks, especially when the target dataset is small.
- **Domain Adaptation:** Transfer learning enables adapting models to new domains or tasks without starting from scratch, making it suitable for various real-world applications.

Conclusion:

Transfer learning and fine-tuning pre-trained models are powerful techniques in deep learning for leveraging knowledge from one task to another. By reusing learned feature representations from pre-trained models and adapting them to new tasks, developers can achieve better performance with less data and computational resources. Understanding the principles and methodologies of transfer learning is essential for effectively applying these techniques to various domains and tasks in deep learning.

Chapter 7: Natural Language Processing with Python

Natural Language Processing (NLP) is a branch of artificial intelligence that focuses on the interaction between computers and human languages. With the advent of deep learning and powerful libraries in Python, such as NLTK (Natural Language Toolkit), spaCy, and Transformers, NLP tasks have become more accessible and efficient to implement. Here's a comprehensive overview of NLP with Python, including its principles, common tasks, and examples:

1. **Principles of NLP:**

Text Processing:

NLP involves processing and analyzing large volumes of text data, including parsing, tokenization, and cleaning.

Tokenization

Tokenization is the process of breaking down text into smaller units, such as words or sentences, which are easier to analyze. This is often the first step in NLP workflows.

Example: Using the NLTK library, a common toolkit for NLP in Python, you can tokenize text into words and sentences as follows:

import nltk

```
nltk.download('punkt') # Download necessary datasets
from nltk.tokenize import word_tokenize, sent_tokenize
text = "Natural Language Processing with Python is fascinating.
It allows for complex text analysis."
print(sent_tokenize(text))
print(word_tokenize(text))
```

This will output lists of sentences and words, respectively, extracted from the input text.

Stop Word Removal

Stop words are common words like "and", "the", "is", etc., which are often removed during the preprocessing phase because they carry little semantic weight.

Example:

```
from nltk.corpus import stopwords
nltk.download('stopwords')
stop_words = set(stopwords.words('english'))
filtered_words = [word for word in word_tokenize(text) if word
not in stop_words]
print(filtered_words)
```

This filters out stop words from the tokenized text, leaving more meaningful words for analysis.

Stemming and Lemmatization

Stemming and lemmatization are techniques used to reduce words to their base or root form. While stemming simply chops off word endings based on common rules, lemmatization involves a more sophisticated analysis to return the base or dictionary form of a word.

Example:

```
from nltk.stem import PorterStemmer, WordNetLemmatizer
nltk.download('wordnet')
stemmer = PorterStemmer()
lemmatizer = WordNetLemmatizer()
word = "running"
```

```
print("Stemmed:", stemmer.stem(word))
print("Lemmatized:", lemmatizer.lemmatize(word, pos='v')) # 'v'
for verb
```

This demonstrates how "running" can be reduced to "run" using both stemming and lemmatization.

Part-of-Speech Tagging

Part-of-speech (POS) tagging involves assigning parts of speech to each word in the text, such as nouns, verbs, adjectives, etc. This is useful for understanding the grammatical structure of sentences.

Example:

```
nltk.download('averaged_perceptron_tagger')
words = word_tokenize("Python is great for NLP.")
print(nltk.pos_tag(words))
```

This will output a list of tuples where each tuple contains a word and its corresponding part of speech.

Named Entity Recognition (NER)

NER is the process of identifying and classifying named entities (e.g., names of people, organizations, locations) within the text. This helps in extracting structured information from unstructured text.

Example:

```
nltk.download('maxent_ne_chunker')
nltk.download('words')
from nltk import ne_chunk
sentence = "Apple Inc. is based in Cupertino."
tags = nltk.pos_tag(word_tokenize(sentence))
entities = ne_chunk(tags)
print(entities)
```

This example identifies "Apple Inc." and "Cupertino" as named entities in the given sentence.

These principles and techniques form the backbone of text processing in NLP and are essential for tasks ranging from sentiment analysis and topic modeling to information retrieval and machine translation. Python, with libraries like NLTK and others such as SpaCy and Gensim, provides a comprehensive and accessible environment for performing sophisticated NLP tasks, making it an invaluable tool for developers and researchers working in the field of natural language processing.

Semantic Understanding:

NLP aims to understand the meaning and context of text, including sentiment analysis, named entity recognition (NER), and topic modeling.

Word Embeddings

Word embeddings are a fundamental technique in NLP for semantic understanding, where words are mapped to vectors of real numbers in a high-dimensional space. This representation captures semantic relationships between words based on their context in a corpus.

Example with Word2Vec (Gensim):

```
from gensim.models import Word2Vec
from nltk.tokenize import word_tokenize
nltk.download('punkt')
sentences = ["Python is a popular programming language.",
"Python is also used for software development.",
"Apart from development, Python supports data analysis."]
# Tokenize sentences
tokenized_sentences = [word_tokenize(sentence.lower()) for sentence in sentences]
# Train a Word2Vec model
model = Word2Vec(sentences=tokenized_sentences, vector_size=100, window=5, min_count=1, workers=4)
vector = model.wv['python'] # Get the vector for 'python'
print(vector)
```

This example demonstrates how to generate word embeddings for words in sentences, capturing the semantic essence of 'python' in the context of programming and data analysis.

Semantic Similarity

Semantic similarity involves measuring the similarity between words or sentences based on their meaning. This is often used in applications like document clustering, information retrieval, and question-answering systems.

Example with SpaCy:

```python
import spacy
# Load a pre-trained model
nlp = spacy.load('en_core_web_md') # Make sure to download this model first
# Process some text
doc1 = nlp("I enjoy sunny weather.")
doc2 = nlp("I like sunny days.")
# Get the similarity between two docs
similarity = doc1.similarity(doc2)
print(f"Semantic similarity: {similarity}")
```

This calculates the semantic similarity between two sentences, demonstrating their closeness in meaning despite differences in wording.

Contextual Word Meanings with BERT

Bidirectional Encoder Representations from Transformers (BERT) and similar models understand the context of words in sentences, allowing for a deeper semantic understanding. These models can differentiate word meanings based on sentence context, improving performance on tasks like sentiment analysis, named entity recognition, and question answering.

Example with Transformers (Hugging Face):

```python
from transformers import BertTokenizer, BertModel
tokenizer = BertTokenizer.from_pretrained('bert-base-uncased')
model = BertModel.from_pretrained('bert-base-uncased')
text = "I went to the bank to withdraw money."
encoded_input = tokenizer(text, return_tensors='pt')
```

```
output = model(**encoded_input)
# The output provides embeddings that capture the contextual
meanings of words
print(output.last_hidden_state)
```

This showcases how BERT processes a sentence to produce embeddings that reflect the contextual meaning of "bank" as a financial institution.

Dependency Parsing

Dependency parsing is another technique for semantic understanding, analyzing the grammatical structure of a sentence to establish relationships between words. It helps in understanding how different parts of a sentence relate to each other semantically.

Example with SpaCy:

```
nlp = spacy.load("en_core_web_sm")
sentence = "The quick brown fox jumps over the lazy dog."
doc = nlp(sentence)
for token in doc:
print(f"{token.text} --> {token.dep_} --> {token.head.text}")
```

This outputs the dependency relations, indicating how words grammatically relate to each other, which is crucial for understanding sentence structure and meaning.

Semantic understanding in NLP with Python encompasses a broad range of techniques from word embeddings to advanced transformer models. These methods enable machines to interpret human language in a way that captures the richness and variability of meaning, paving the way for sophisticated applications that require a deep understanding of text. Python's NLP libraries, such as NLTK, Gensim, SpaCy, and Hugging Face's Transformers, provide accessible and powerful tools for developers and researchers to explore and leverage semantic understanding in their projects.

Language Generation:

NLP techniques are used for text generation tasks such as machine translation, text summarization, and chatbots.

Language Models

At the heart of language generation are language models, which are statistical models that learn the probability of word sequences in a language. These models can predict the likelihood of the next word in a sentence based on the previous words, enabling the generation of text.

Example: Building a simple bigram model with Python's NLTK library:

```
from nltk import bigrams, FreqDist, ConditionalFreqDist
from nltk.tokenize import word_tokenize
text = "Python is widely used in natural language processing. Language generation with Python is fascinating."
tokens = word_tokenize(text)
bigram_measures = bigrams(tokens)
# Frequency distribution of bigrams
bigram_freq = FreqDist(bigram_measures)
# Conditional frequency distribution of words
cfd = ConditionalFreqDist(bigram_freq)
# Predict the next word
word = 'Python'
predicted_words = cfd[word].most_common(2) # Get two most common next words
print(predicted_words)
```

This simple model can predict the next word following 'Python' based on its learned bigram frequencies.

Seq2Seq Models and Attention Mechanisms

Sequence-to-Sequence (Seq2Seq) models, particularly with the incorporation of attention mechanisms, have significantly advanced the field of language generation. These models are adept at translating input sequences (words, letters, or features) into output sequences, making them ideal for tasks like machine translation, text summarization, and question-answering.

Example: Although implementing a Seq2Seq model from scratch is beyond a simple code snippet due to its complexity, Python's TensorFlow and PyTorch libraries provide high-level APIs for building these models. Here's a conceptual outline:

Pseudocode for Seq2Seq with attention in PyTorch

Define the encoder network

class EncoderRNN(nn.Module):

initialization and forward pass

Define the decoder network with attention

class AttnDecoderRNN(nn.Module):

initialization and forward pass

Training and generating sequences

1. Pass the input sequence through the encoder.

2. Use encoder's output and internal state as initial decoder input.

3. Decoder uses previous predictions as inputs for next step prediction.

This highlights the structure of a Seq2Seq model with attention, where the encoder processes the input sequence, and the decoder generates the output sequence, with attention mechanisms improving context awareness.

Transformers and Pretrained Models

Transformers have revolutionized NLP, offering remarkable improvements in language generation tasks. Pretrained models like GPT (Generative Pretrained Transformer) and BERT (Bidirectional Encoder Representations from Transformers) leverage vast amounts of text data to generate coherent and contextually rich text.

Example: Using the Hugging Face Transformers library to generate text with GPT-2:

from transformers import GPT2Tokenizer, GPT2LMHeadModel

```
# Load pre-trained model and tokenizer
model = GPT2LMHeadModel.from_pretrained('gpt2')
tokenizer = GPT2Tokenizer.from_pretrained('gpt2')
# Encode input context and generate sequence
inputs = tokenizer.encode("The future of Python in natural language processing", return_tensors='pt')
outputs = model.generate(inputs, max_length=50, num_return_sequences=1)
# Decode and print the generated text
print(tokenizer.decode(outputs[0], skip_special_tokens=True)).
```

This generates text that follows from the provided input context, showcasing the capability of pretrained models in language generation.

Language generation in NLP is a complex but fascinating area, and Python provides an excellent platform for exploring and implementing these technologies. From simple statistical models to advanced neural networks and transformers, Python's libraries like NLTK, TensorFlow, PyTorch, and Transformers offer the tools needed to push the boundaries of what's possible in automated language generation. Whether for creating engaging chatbot responses, generating articles, or summarizing content, Python's ecosystem enables developers and researchers to innovate and implement cutting-edge solutions in the realm of natural language generation.

Statistical Modeling:

Many NLP tasks involve applying statistical models and machine learning algorithms to analyze and process text data effectively.

N-gram Models

N-gram models are fundamental statistical models that predict the next item in a sequence (e.g., a word in a sentence) based on the history of previous items. An n-gram is a contiguous sequence of n items from a given sample of text or speech.

Example: Building a simple bigram (2-gram) model using

Python's NLTK library to predict the next word:

```python
import nltk
from nltk import bigrams, ConditionalFreqDist
text = "Python is widely used in natural language processing. Natural language processing with Python is fascinating."
tokens = nltk.word_tokenize(text)
bigrams = bigrams(tokens)
cfd = ConditionalFreqDist(bigrams)
# Predict the next word after "language"
predicted_word = cfd["language"].max()
print(predicted_word)
```

This model uses the frequency of bigram occurrences to predict the most likely word to follow a given word, in this case, predicting the word after "language".

TF-IDF (Term Frequency-Inverse Document Frequency)

TF-IDF is a statistical measure used to evaluate the importance of a word in a document relative to a corpus. This technique is widely used in information retrieval and text mining.

Example: Calculating TF-IDF scores for words in documents using Python's **TfidfVectorizer** from the scikit-learn library:

```python
from sklearn.feature_extraction.text import TfidfVectorizer
documents = [
"Python is used in machine learning.",
"Python and natural language processing are closely related.",
"Machine learning applications are diverse."
]
vectorizer = TfidfVectorizer()
tfidf_matrix = vectorizer.fit_transform(documents)
# Get the first document's TF-IDF scores
feature_names = vectorizer.get_feature_names_out()
first_document_tfidf = tfidf_matrix[0].T.todense()
df = pd.DataFrame(first_document_tfidf, index=feature_names, columns=["TF-IDF"])
```

```
df = df.sort_values('TF-IDF', ascending=False)
print(df.head())
```

This calculates the TF-IDF scores for each word in the documents, highlighting the importance of each word within the document set.

Naive Bayes Classifier for Text Classification

The Naive Bayes classifier is a probabilistic model based on Bayes' Theorem with the "naive" assumption of independence between features. It's particularly effective in text classification tasks, such as spam detection or sentiment analysis.

Example: Implementing a simple Naive Bayes classifier for sentiment analysis using the NLTK library:

```
from nltk.classify import NaiveBayesClassifier
from nltk.sentiment import SentimentAnalyzer
from nltk.sentiment.util import *
# Sample positive and negative sentences
positive_sentences = [('I love Python programming.', 'pos')]
negative_sentences = [('I hate rainy days.', 'neg')]
# Extract unigram features
sentim_analyzer = SentimentAnalyzer()
all_words_neg = sentim_analyzer.all_words([mark_negation(doc) for doc in negative_sentences])
unigram_feats = sentim_analyzer.unigram_word_feats(all_words_neg, min_freq=4)
sentim_analyzer.add_feat_extractor(extract_unigram_feats, unigrams=unigram_feats)
# Train the Naive Bayes classifier
training_set = sentim_analyzer.apply_features(positive_sentences + negative_sentences)
trainer = NaiveBayesClassifier.train
classifier = sentim_analyzer.train(trainer, training_set)
# Classify a new sentence
test_sentence = "Python is amazing."
test_sent_features = sentim_analyzer.extract_features(test_sen-
```

tence.split())

print(classifier.classify(test_sent_features))

This example trains a Naive Bayes classifier to distinguish between positive and negative sentiments and then classifies a new sentence.

Statistical modeling in NLP provides a robust framework for understanding and generating human language. Through the application of models like n-grams, TF-IDF, and Naive Bayes classifiers, Python enables developers and researchers to tackle a wide array of NLP tasks, from text classification and sentiment analysis to language generation and beyond. Python's libraries, such as NLTK and scikit-learn, offer the tools and flexibility needed to implement these statistical models effectively, making Python a powerful ally in the realm of NLP.

2. **Common NLP Tasks:**

Tokenization:

Tokenization is a fundamental task in Natural Language Processing (NLP) that involves breaking down text into smaller units, such as words, sentences, or phrases, known as tokens. This process is crucial for preparing text data for further analysis or processing in various NLP tasks like sentiment analysis, text classification, machine translation, and more. Python, with its rich ecosystem of NLP libraries, provides efficient and accessible tools for performing tokenization. Below, we explore how tokenization is approached in NLP using Python, including practical examples to illustrate its application.

Word Tokenization

Word tokenization divides text into individual words or terms. It's a preliminary step for many NLP applications, enabling the analysis and processing of text at the word level.

Example with NLTK:

import nltk

from nltk.tokenize import word_tokenize

```
nltk.download('punkt') # Download necessary datasets
text = "Python is a powerful programming language."
tokens = word_tokenize(text)
print(tokens)
```

This will output a list of words: **['Python', 'is', 'a', 'powerful', 'programming', 'language', '.']**.

Example with spaCy:

```
import spacy
nlp = spacy.load("en_core_web_sm") # Load the English tokenizer
text = "Python is a powerful programming language."
doc = nlp(text)
tokens = [token.text for token in doc]
print(tokens)
```

spaCy also provides word tokenization, yielding a similar output, showcasing its comprehensive linguistic annotations.

Sentence Tokenization

Sentence tokenization, or sentence segmentation, breaks text down into individual sentences. This is particularly useful in tasks that require an understanding of the complete thought or in applications like summarization where sentence boundaries are crucial.

Example with NLTK:

```
from nltk.tokenize import sent_tokenize
text = "Python is popular for NLP. It has many libraries for text processing."
sentences = sent_tokenize(text)
print(sentences)
```

This outputs the sentences as individual strings in a list: **['Python is popular for NLP.', 'It has many libraries for text processing.']**.

Example with spaCy:

```
text = "Python is popular for NLP. It has many libraries for text
```

processing."
doc = nlp(text)
sentences = [sent.text for sent in doc.sents]
print(sentences)

In spaCy, the **doc.sents** property provides a division of the document into sentences.

Subword Tokenization

Subword tokenization splits words into smaller components (subwords or characters), beneficial for handling unknown words, morphologically rich languages, or in neural network models where input size is a constraint.

Example with Hugging Face's Tokenizers:

from tokenizers import Tokenizer
from tokenizers.models import BPE
tokenizer = Tokenizer(BPE())
tokenizer.train(["path/to/your/dataset.txt"])
encoded = tokenizer.encode("Tokenization with Python.")
print(encoded.tokens)

This demonstrates training a Byte Pair Encoding (BPE) tokenizer on a dataset, a common subword tokenization method, and encoding a sample sentence.

Tokenization is a critical step in the preprocessing phase of many NLP tasks, serving as the foundation for transforming raw text into a structured form that algorithms can interpret. Python's NLP libraries like NLTK, spaCy, and Hugging Face's Tokenizers provide robust and efficient tools for performing various tokenization techniques, catering to the diverse needs of NLP applications. Whether dealing with word-level, sentence-level, or subword-level tokenization, Python offers the flexibility and resources necessary for effective text analysis and processing.

Part-of-Speech (POS) Tagging:

Part-of-Speech (POS) Tagging is an essential task in Natural Language Processing (NLP) that involves identifying each word's part of speech in a text, such as nouns, verbs, adjectives, etc. This process is crucial for understanding the grammatical structure of sentences and is foundational for further NLP tasks like parsing, named entity recognition, and even in contributing to the effectiveness of machine translation and sentiment analysis. Python, renowned for its NLP capabilities, offers various libraries that facilitate POS tagging with considerable ease and accuracy.

NLTK: Natural Language Toolkit

NLTK is one of the most widely-used Python libraries for NLP. It provides a simple interface to over 50 corpora and lexical resources such as WordNet, along with a suite of text processing libraries for classification, tokenization, stemming, tagging, and parsing.

Example of POS Tagging with NLTK:

```python
import nltk
from nltk.tokenize import word_tokenize
nltk.download('averaged_perceptron_tagger')
text = "Python is an excellent language for NLP."
words = word_tokenize(text)
pos_tags = nltk.pos_tag(words)
print(pos_tags)
```

This code snippet tokenizes a sentence into words and then uses **nltk.pos_tag** to assign POS tags to each token. The output is a list of tuples, where each tuple contains a word and its corresponding POS tag.

spaCy: Industrial-Strength NLP

spaCy is another powerful library for NLP in Python that excels in large-scale information extraction tasks. It's designed for practical, real-world tasks with a focus on performance and efficiency. spaCy provides pre-trained models for various languages, capable of performing multiple NLP tasks including POS tagging.

Example of POS Tagging with spaCy:

```
import spacy
nlp = spacy.load("en_core_web_sm")
text = "Python is an excellent language for NLP."
doc = nlp(text)
for token in doc:
print(token.text, token.pos_)
```

Upon processing the text, each **Token** object in the **Doc** container has attributes that provide the POS tag (**pos_**). The output is similar to NLTK but spaCy provides additional features and attributes for each token.

Universal POS Tags

Both NLTK and spaCy use the Penn Treebank POS Tagset for English, which is specific to that corpus. However, there's a move towards using Universal POS tags, a simplified set of POS tags designed for use across different languages. This standardization facilitates comparative linguistics studies and the development of multilingual applications.

Application in Text Analysis

POS tagging plays a vital role in syntactic and semantic analysis, influencing the performance of many higher-level NLP tasks. For example:

Syntax Parsing: POS tags are used as inputs for parsing algorithms to construct syntactic trees, which represent the grammatical structure of sentences.

Named Entity Recognition (NER): POS tags help in identifying proper nouns that could be potential named entities.

Sentiment Analysis: Adjectives identified through POS tagging can be crucial indicators of sentiment in text.

POS tagging is a fundamental NLP task that serves as a stepping stone for more complex analyses and applications. Python's NLP libraries like NLTK and spaCy provide robust tools for accurate and efficient POS tagging, suitable for both academic research and industrial applications. Understanding the grammatical structure of text through POS tagging opens up possibilities for deeper linguistic insights and more nuanced text processing capabilities, highlighting the importance of this task in the broader NLP landscape.

Named Entity Recognition (NER):

Named Entity Recognition (NER) is a pivotal task in Natural Language Processing (NLP) that involves identifying and classifying key elements in text into predefined categories such as the names of persons, organizations, locations, expressions of times, quantities, monetary values, percentages, etc. NER is crucial for information extraction, content classification, question answering systems, and knowledge base construction, among other applications. Python, being a leading language in NLP, offers robust libraries equipped with NER capabilities.

spaCy: High-Performance NER

spaCy is a modern and fast NLP library that provides pre-trained models for NER among its various capabilities. spaCy's models are trained on a large corpus and can identify a wide range of named entities.

Example of NER with spaCy:

```python
import spacy
# Load a pre-trained model
nlp = spacy.load("en_core_web_sm")
# Process a text
text = "Apple Inc. announced the new iPhone at their headquarters in Cupertino."
doc = nlp(text)
# Extract entities
for ent in doc.ents:
print(ent.text, ent.label_)
```

This example processes a text through spaCy's NLP pipeline, extracting named entities and their labels. spaCy identifies "Apple Inc." as an organization, "iPhone" as a product, and "Cupertino" as a location.

NLTK: Versatile NER with Chunking

NLTK provides a more manual approach to NER, which can be customized with chunking. Chunking is a process of extracting phrases from unstructured text and classifying them into predefined categories. While NLTK includes a named entity chunker, its capabilities are more basic compared to spaCy's.

Example of NER with NLTK:

```python
import nltk
from nltk import ne_chunk
from nltk.tokenize import word_tokenize
nltk.download('maxent_ne_chunker')
nltk.download('words')
nltk.download('punkt')
text = "Microsoft was founded by Bill Gates and Paul Allen."
tokens = word_tokenize(text)
tags = nltk.pos_tag(tokens)
tree = ne_chunk(tags)
print(tree)
```

This code tokenizes the text, tags each token with part-of-speech tags, and then uses **ne_chunk** to identify named entities. The output is a tree structure with named entities identified.

Transformers: State-of-the-Art NER

The **transformers** library by Hugging Face includes state-of-the-art NER models based on transformer architectures like BERT, GPT, and RoBERTa. These models, pre-trained on vast text corpora, can be fine-tuned for specific NER tasks and offer superior accuracy.

Example of NER with Transformers:

```python
from transformers import pipeline
# Load a pre-trained NER pipeline
ner_pipeline = pipeline("ner", model="dbmdz/bert-large-cased-finetuned-conll03-english")
```

text = "Angela Merkel and Barack Obama spoke in Berlin."
results = ner_pipeline(text)
for entity in results:
print(entity['word'], entity['entity'])
This example utilizes a pre-trained BERT model fine-tuned on the CoNLL-03 dataset, capable of extracting and classifying named entities with high accuracy. The pipeline identifies "Angela Merkel" and "Barack Obama" as persons and "Berlin" as a location.

Named Entity Recognition is a crucial component of NLP applications that necessitate understanding and extracting key information from text. Python's rich ecosystem of NLP libraries like spaCy, NLTK, and Transformers provides a range of options from simple, rule-based approaches to advanced, neural network-based models for performing NER. Depending on the requirements of the task, developers can choose the library that best fits their needs, leveraging Python's capabilities to implement efficient and accurate NER systems.

Sentiment Analysis:

Sentiment Analysis, often referred to as opinion mining, is a pivotal task in Natural Language Processing (NLP) that involves determining the emotional tone behind a body of text. This is a key aspect of understanding human emotions, enabling businesses and researchers to gauge public opinion, monitor brand and product sentiment, and conduct market research, among other applications. Python, with its comprehensive suite of NLP libraries, stands at the forefront of sentiment analysis, offering tools that range from simple lexicon-based approaches to sophisticated neural network models.

TextBlob: Simple Lexicon-Based Sentiment Analysis

TextBlob is a Python library that offers a simple API for common NLP tasks, including sentiment analysis. It uses a lexicon of pre-assigned scores for words and phrases that indicate positivity, negativity, and subjectivity.

Example of Sentiment Analysis with TextBlob:

```
from textblob import TextBlob
text = "Python is an amazing programming language!"
blob = TextBlob(text)
# Get the sentiment polarity
print(blob.sentiment.polarity)
```

This code snippet evaluates the sentiment polarity of a text, where the polarity score ranges from -1 (very negative) to 1 (very positive). TextBlob also provides a subjectivity score, which ranges from 0 (very objective) to 1 (very subjective).

VADER: Sentiment Analysis for Social Media

VADER (Valence Aware Dictionary and sEntiment Reasoner) is a lexicon and rule-based sentiment analysis tool that is specifically attuned to sentiments expressed in social media. It is available in the NLTK library and is particularly effective for texts that contain slang, emojis, and abbreviations.

Example of Sentiment Analysis with VADER:

```
import nltk
from nltk.sentiment import SentimentIntensityAnalyzer
nltk.download('vader_lexicon')
text = "I love Python! :)"
sia = SentimentIntensityAnalyzer()
print(sia.polarity_scores(text))
```

This returns a dictionary with polarity scores for the text, providing a compound score that aggregates the computed negativity, neutrality, and positivity scores to represent the overall sentiment.

spaCy: Utilizing Machine Learning Models

spaCy, known for its robust NLP capabilities, can be extended with additional libraries like **spacytextblob** for sentiment analysis. While spaCy itself does not provide a built-in sentiment analysis feature, its powerful processing pipeline facilitates the integration of machine learning models for custom sentiment analysis tasks.

Example of Extending spaCy for Sentiment Analysis:

```
import spacy
from spacytextblob.spacytextblob import SpacyTextBlob
nlp = spacy.load("en_core_web_sm")
nlp.add_pipe('spacytextblob')
text = "Python makes me happy."
doc = nlp(text)
print(doc._.sentiment.polarity)
```

This setup integrates TextBlob's sentiment analysis into spaCy's pipeline, offering an easy way to apply sentiment analysis within spaCy's comprehensive NLP framework.

Transformers: State-of-the-Art Sentiment Analysis

The **transformers** library provides access to state-of-the-art models like BERT, GPT-2, and RoBERTa, which can be fine-tuned for sentiment analysis, offering high accuracy and the ability to understand the context better than simple lexicon-based methods.

Example of Sentiment Analysis with Transformers:

```
from transformers import pipeline
# Load a pre-trained sentiment analysis pipeline
sentiment_pipeline = pipeline("sentiment-analysis")
text = "I've always enjoyed learning new things, and Python offers endless possibilities."
result = sentiment_pipeline(text)
print(result)
```

This utilizes a pre-trained model specialized in sentiment analysis to evaluate the sentiment of the provided text, demonstrating the power of transformer models in capturing nuanced sentiments.

Sentiment analysis in Python enables the extraction of emotional insights from text data through a variety of approaches, from simple lexicon-based methods to advanced deep learning models. Libraries like TextBlob, VADER, spaCy, and Transformers provide the tools needed to implement sentiment analysis effectively, catering to a wide range of applications. Whether for analyzing customer feedback, monitoring social media sentiment, or conducting market research, Python's NLP ecosystem offers powerful solutions for sentiment analysis tasks.

Text Classification:

Text classification, also known as text categorization, is a fundamental task in Natural Language Processing (NLP) where a body of text is assigned to one or more predefined categories. This task underpins a variety of applications, such as spam detection in emails, sentiment analysis in social media, topic labeling of news articles, and document organization in databases. Python, with its rich ecosystem of NLP and machine learning libraries, is a powerful tool for implementing text classification solutions.

scikit-learn: Machine Learning in Python

Scikit-learn is a versatile Python library for machine learning that provides simple and efficient tools for data analysis and modeling. It's particularly well-suited for text classification tasks, offering a range of algorithms and utilities for preprocessing text data, extracting features, and training classifiers.

Example of Text Classification with scikit-learn:

```
from sklearn.feature_extraction.text import TfidfVectorizer
from sklearn.naive_bayes import MultinomialNB
from sklearn.pipeline import make_pipeline
# Sample text data and labels
texts = [
"Python is a powerful programming language.",
"Machine learning can be fascinating.",
"Python is used in machine learning.",
"Spam emails are annoying."
]
```

```python
labels = ['python', 'ml', 'python', 'spam']
# Create a pipeline that vectorizes the text, then applies a Naive Bayes classifier
model = make_pipeline(TfidfVectorizer(), MultinomialNB())
# Train the model
model.fit(texts, labels)
# Predict the category of a new text
predicted_label = model.predict(["Python is frequently used in data science."])[0]
print(predicted_label)
```

This example demonstrates how to use a TF-IDF vectorizer to convert text into a format suitable for machine learning, and then apply a Naive Bayes classifier to predict the category of new text.

spaCy: Industrial-Strength NLP

spaCy is another powerful library for NLP in Python, designed for production use. It supports deep learning workflows and integrates with libraries like TensorFlow and PyTorch. While spaCy provides foundational tools for text classification, it excels when used in conjunction with a neural network library for more complex models.

Example of Text Classification with spaCy:

```python
import spacy
from spacy.util import minibatch
import random
# Load a pre-existing spacy model
nlp = spacy.blank("en")
# Create a text classifier with exclusive classes and add it to the pipeline
textcat = nlp.create_pipe("textcat", config={"exclusive_classes": True})
nlp.add_pipe(textcat)
# Add labels to the text classifier
textcat.add_label("PYTHON")
```

```
textcat.add_label("ML")
textcat.add_label("SPAM")
# Training data
train_texts = texts
train_labels = [{'cats': {'PYTHON': label == 'python', 'ML': label
== 'ml', 'SPAM': label == 'spam'}} for label in labels]
# Use minibatch to speed up the training
batches = minibatch(list(zip(train_texts, train_labels)), size=2)
# Update the model
optimizer = nlp.begin_training()
for batch in batches:
texts, annotations = zip(*batch)
nlp.update(texts, annotations, sgd=optimizer)
# Test the trained model
test_text = "Python has extensive libraries for data analysis."
doc = nlp(test_text)
print(max(doc.cats, key=doc.cats.get))
```

This setup involves creating a text categorizer pipeline in spaCy, adding category labels, and training the model with example texts. It showcases how to build a custom text classification model with spaCy.

Transformers: Leveraging Pretrained Models

The **transformers** library by Hugging Face provides access to state-of-the-art pretrained models that can be fine-tuned for specific tasks, including text classification. Models like BERT, GPT, and RoBERTa have achieved remarkable results on a variety of NLP benchmarks.

Example of Text Classification with Transformers:

```
from transformers import pipeline
# Load a pre-trained sentiment analysis pipeline
classifier = pipeline("text-classification", model="distilbert-base-
uncased-finetuned-sst-2-english")
# Predict the category of a new text
```

```
print(classifier("I love using Python for my data science
projects."))
```

This utilizes a pre-trained DistilBERT model fine-tuned for sentiment analysis, illustrating the process of text classification with just a few lines of code. The **transformers** pipeline abstraction simplifies the application of these powerful models to custom text classification tasks.

Text classification is a versatile and widely applicable NLP task that benefits from Python's extensive selection of libraries and tools. Whether through traditional machine learning techniques with scikit-learn, deep learning models with spaCy and neural network libraries, or state-of-the-art pretrained models with the **transformers** library, Python equips developers and data scientists with the capabilities needed to implement effective text classification solutions across a range of domains.

Topic Modeling:

Topic modeling is a sophisticated Natural Language Processing (NLP) task aimed at discovering the abstract topics that pervade a collection of documents. It's particularly useful in digital libraries, content management, and information retrieval to enhance search and navigation. By uncovering hidden thematic structures, topic modeling provides insights into large volumes of text data, making it invaluable for summarizing, understanding, and organizing content. Python, with its rich ecosystem for data science and NLP, offers several libraries and tools that facilitate topic modeling.

Latent Dirichlet Allocation (LDA) with Gensim

Latent Dirichlet Allocation (LDA) is one of the most popular topic modeling techniques. It assumes that each document is a mixture of a small number of topics and that each word's presence is attributable to one of the document's topics. Gensim is a Python library designed to handle large text collections, using efficient algorithms to extract semantic topics.

Example of Topic Modeling with LDA in Gensim:

```python
from gensim import corpora, models
from nltk.tokenize import word_tokenize
# Sample documents
documents = [
"Python is a powerful programming language.",
"Python can be used in data science projects.",
"Data science is an exciting field.",
"Machine learning is a part of data science."
]
# Tokenize the documents
tokenized_docs = [word_tokenize(doc.lower()) for doc in documents]
# Create a dictionary representation of the documents
dictionary = corpora.Dictionary(tokenized_docs)
# Convert dictionary to a bag of words corpus
corpus = [dictionary.doc2bow(doc) for doc in tokenized_docs]
# Apply LDA
lda_model = models.LdaModel(corpus, num_topics=2, id2word=dictionary, passes=15)
# Print topics
topics = lda_model.print_topics(num_words=4)
for topic in topics:
print(topic)
```

This code tokenizes the documents, creates a dictionary and corpus, and then applies LDA to generate topics. The **print_topics** method displays the most significant words in each topic.

Non-negative Matrix Factorization (NMF) with scikit-learn

Non-negative Matrix Factorization (NMF) is another technique for topic modeling that factorizes the original document-word matrix into lower-dimensional matrices, revealing the topics. Scikit-learn, a machine learning library in Python, provides an implementation of NMF that can be used for topic modeling.

Example of Topic Modeling with NMF in scikit-learn:

```python
from sklearn.feature_extraction.text import TfidfVectorizer
from sklearn.decomposition import NMF
import numpy as np
# Sample documents (same as above)
documents = [
"Python is a powerful programming language.",
"Python can be used in data science projects.",
"Data science is an exciting field.",
"Machine learning is a part of data science."
]
# Create a TF-IDF Vectorizer
tfidf_vectorizer = TfidfVectorizer(max_df=0.95, min_df=2, stop_words='english')
tfidf = tfidf_vectorizer.fit_transform(documents)
# Apply NMF
nmf_model = NMF(n_components=2, random_state=1)
nmf = nmf_model.fit_transform(tfidf)
# Print topics
feature_names = tfidf_vectorizer.get_feature_names_out()
for topic_idx, topic in enumerate(nmf_model.components_):
print("Topic #%d:" % topic_idx)
print(" ".join([feature_names[i] for i in topic.argsort()[:-4 - 1:-1]]))
```

This example uses TF-IDF for vectorization and applies NMF to extract topics, displaying the most significant words for each topic.

Topic Modeling Evaluation

Evaluating topic models can be challenging due to the unsupervised nature of the algorithms. Common approaches include coherence scores, which measure the degree of semantic similarity between high-scoring words in the topic, and perplexity, which measures how well the model predicts a sample. Gensim provides functions to compute coherence scores, offering a quantitative way to assess and compare the performance of different topic models or configurations.

Topic modeling is a powerful technique in NLP for extracting insightful themes from large collections of text data. Python, through libraries like Gensim and scikit-learn, provides accessible and efficient tools for performing topic modeling, enabling the discovery of latent topics in text. Whether through LDA, NMF, or other algorithms, topic modeling in Python helps uncover the underlying thematic structure of document collections, facilitating content analysis, organization, and retrieval tasks across various domains.

Machine Translation:

Machine Translation (MT) is a complex and fascinating task in Natural Language Processing (NLP) that focuses on automatically translating text or speech from one language to another. It encompasses a variety of techniques, from rule-based methods to statistical models and, more recently, neural network approaches that have significantly improved translation quality. Python, with its robust NLP and machine learning ecosystem, offers a powerful platform for developing and deploying machine translation systems.

Statistical Machine Translation (SMT)

Statistical Machine Translation (SMT) relies on statistical models where the parameters are derived from the analysis of bilingual text corpora. The core idea is that the likelihood of translation is determined based on the alignment of words in parallel corpora.

NLTK Example:

While Python's NLTK library is more renowned for its comprehensive suite of linguistic tools, it also offers basic functionalities for statistical machine translation, such as alignment models and bilingual corpora.

Note: NLTK provides basic tools for SMT but is not optimized

for high-performance translation tasks.

```
import nltk
nltk.download('comtrans')
# Assume availability of a parallel corpus and a simplistic approach to demonstrate SMT concepts
# For practical SMT applications, consider using specialized libraries like Moses for complex pipeline construction.
```

For serious SMT projects, tools like Moses offer a more comprehensive environment for training and applying statistical models, though interfacing with such tools typically extends beyond Python.

Neural Machine Translation (NMT)

Neural Machine Translation represents a significant advancement in MT, leveraging deep neural networks to model the entire translation process end-to-end. This approach has surpassed traditional statistical methods in terms of translation quality, especially with the advent of sequence-to-sequence (seq2seq) models and attention mechanisms.

TensorFlow and PyTorch Example:

Both TensorFlow and PyTorch are popular frameworks for building neural machine translation systems due to their support for deep learning architectures.

```
# Pseudocode for NMT with TensorFlow or PyTorch
from tensorflow.keras.models import Model
from tensorflow.keras.layers import Input, LSTM, Dense
# or
import torch
import torch.nn as nn
# Define your seq2seq model architecture here
# Training an NMT model requires a significant amount of data and computational resources
# For detailed implementations, refer to TensorFlow's or PyTorch's documentation and tutorials on NMT.
```

Transformers for Machine Translation

The introduction of the Transformer model has revolutionized NMT, offering superior translation quality with more parallelizable computations. Libraries like Hugging Face's Transformers provide access to pre-trained Transformer models like BERT, GPT, and T5, which can be fine-tuned for machine translation tasks.

Hugging Face Transformers Example:

```
from transformers import pipeline
# Load a pre-trained translation pipeline
translator = pipeline("translation_en_to_fr", model="t5-base")
# Translate text from English to French
translation = translator("Python is a powerful programming language for NLP.", max_length=40)
print(translation[0]['translation_text'])
```

This example demonstrates using a pre-trained T5 model for translating English text into French, showcasing the ease of using Transformer models for machine translation with Python.

Evaluation of Machine Translation

Evaluating the quality of machine translations is critical for developing effective MT systems. BLEU (Bilingual Evaluation Understudy) is a widely used metric that compares machine-generated translations with one or more reference translations. Python libraries like SacreBLEU offer standardized BLEU score computation.

Machine translation is a key application of NLP that has seen remarkable progress with the advent of neural network-based models. Python, through its extensive libraries and frameworks, provides a fertile ground for exploring and implementing cutting-edge MT systems. From statistical models to advanced neural architectures like Transformers, Python enables developers and researchers to push the boundaries of what's possible in automatic language translation, bridging linguistic gaps and facilitating global communication.

Text Generation:

Text generation is a captivating domain within Natural Language Processing (NLP) that involves creating coherent and contextually relevant text based on given input. It spans a variety of applications, including chatbots, content creation, automated storytelling, and more. Python, renowned for its comprehensive NLP capabilities, offers a plethora of libraries and frameworks that facilitate the exploration and implementation of text generation models.

Markov Chains for Simple Text Generation

Markov chains can be utilized for generating text by building a model that predicts the next word in a sequence based on the current state or word. This method, while simple, can produce surprisingly coherent results for short text sequences.

Example with basic Python:

```python
import random
def build_markov_chain(text, chain={}):
words = text.split(' ')
index = 1
for word in words[index:]:
key = words[index - 1]
if key in chain:
chain[key].append(word)
else:
chain[key] = [word]
index += 1
return chain
def generate_sentence(chain, count=15):
word1 = random.choice(list(chain.keys()))
sentence = word1.capitalize()
for i in range(count-1):
word2 = random.choice(chain[word1])
```

```
word1 = word2
sentence += ' ' + word2
sentence += '.'
return sentence
text = "Python is amazing. It allows for complex text generation. Text generation with Python is fun."
chain = build_markov_chain(text)
print(generate_sentence(chain))
```

This basic example constructs a Markov chain from the input text and then generates a new sentence based on the chain.

Recurrent Neural Networks (RNN) for Text Generation

Recurrent Neural Networks, particularly LSTM (Long Short-Term Memory) networks, have been pivotal in advancing text generation. They can capture long-term dependencies in text data, making them suitable for generating more coherent and contextually relevant text.

Example with TensorFlow/Keras:

```
from tensorflow.keras.models import Sequential
from tensorflow.keras.layers import LSTM, Dense, Embedding
# Assuming preprocessing has been done to convert text to sequences
model = Sequential()
model.add(Embedding(input_dim=vocab_size, output_dim=50, input_length=sequence_length))
model.add(LSTM(100, return_sequences=False))
model.add(Dense(vocab_size, activation='softmax'))
model.compile(loss='categorical_crossentropy', optimizer='adam')
# model.fit(X, y, epochs=20) # Training model on the dataset
# Generate text...
```

This snippet outlines creating an LSTM model for text generation, focusing on the model's architecture. The actual training and text generation involve additional steps, including data preprocessing and decoding the model's predictions.

Transformers for Advanced Text Generation

Transformers, introduced by the paper "Attention is All You Need," have set new standards for text generation, surpassing RNNs and LSTMs in performance. The GPT (Generative Pre-trained Transformer) series, in particular, has demonstrated remarkable capabilities in generating human-like text.

Example with Hugging Face's Transformers:

```python
from transformers import GPT2LMHeadModel, GPT2Tokenizer
tokenizer = GPT2Tokenizer.from_pretrained('gpt2')
model = GPT2LMHeadModel.from_pretrained('gpt2')
input_text = "The future of Python in NLP is"
input_ids = tokenizer.encode(input_text, return_tensors='pt')
output = model.generate(input_ids, max_length=50, num_beams=5, early_stopping=True)
print(tokenizer.decode(output[0], skip_special_tokens=True))
```

This code utilizes the pre-trained GPT-2 model to generate text following the provided input prompt, showcasing the power of Transformers in text generation tasks.

Evaluation and Challenges

Evaluating the quality of generated text remains a challenge, with metrics like BLEU (for translation tasks) and perplexity often used, though they may not fully capture human judgments of coherence and creativity. Moreover, ensuring ethical use and preventing the generation of harmful or biased content are significant considerations in text generation applications.

Text generation encompasses a broad range of techniques, from simple Markov chains to advanced neural network models like RNNs and Transformers. Python's rich ecosystem, including TensorFlow, Keras, and Hugging Face's Transformers library, offers a powerful toolkit for developing text generation systems. As models and methodologies continue to evolve, Python remains at the forefront of enabling creative and innovative applications in automated text generation.

3. **Example NLP Tasks with Python:**

Tokenization with NLTK:

```
from nltk.tokenize import word_tokenize
text = "Natural Language Processing is fun!"
tokens = word_tokenize(text)
print(tokens)
```

Sentiment Analysis with spaCy:

```
import spacy
from spacytextblob import TextBlob
nlp = spacy.load('en_core_web_sm')
text = "I love NLP and Python!"
doc = nlp(text)
print(doc._.polarity)
```

Named Entity Recognition (NER) with Transformers:

```
from transformers import pipeline
nlp = pipeline("ner")
text = "Apple Inc. is headquartered in Cupertino, California."
entities = nlp(text)
print(entities)
```

4. **Popular NLP Libraries in Python:**

NLTK (Natural Language Toolkit):

The Natural Language Toolkit (NLTK) is one of the most popular and foundational libraries for Natural Language Processing (NLP) in Python. It provides easy access to over 50 corpora and lexical resources such as WordNet, along with a suite of libraries for classification, tokenization, stemming, tagging, parsing, and semantic reasoning. This makes NLTK an indispensable tool for educators, researchers, and developers venturing into NLP.

Tokenization

Tokenization is a basic yet crucial step in NLP that involves splitting text into words, phrases, symbols, or other meaningful elements called tokens. NLTK offers comprehensive functions for both word and sentence tokenization.

Example of Tokenization:

from nltk.tokenize import word_tokenize, sent_tokenize

text = "NLTK is a leading platform for building Python programs to work with human language data. It provides easy-to-use interfaces."

print(sent_tokenize(text))

print(word_tokenize(text))

This example demonstrates splitting the text into sentences and then into words, showcasing the ease with which text can be tokenized for further processing.

Part-of-Speech (POS) Tagging

After tokenization, understanding the role of each word in a sentence is often necessary. POS tagging assigns parts of speech to each word (such as noun, verb, adjective, etc.), based on its definition and context.

Example of POS Tagging:

from nltk import pos_tag

from nltk.tokenize import word_tokenize

text = "NLTK has been used successfully as a teaching tool, as an individual study tool, and as a platform for prototyping and building research systems."

tokens = word_tokenize(text)

pos_tags = pos_tag(tokens)

print(pos_tags)

This code tokenizes the input text and then applies POS tagging, demonstrating NLTK's capability to provide grammatical information about each token.

Named Entity Recognition (NER)

Named Entity Recognition identifies and classifies named entities (people, organizations, locations, etc.) in text into predefined categories. NLTK offers functions to perform NER using a pre-trained model.

Example of NER:

```
from nltk import ne_chunk, pos_tag
from nltk.tokenize import word_tokenize
from nltk.tree import Tree
text = "Microsoft Corporation was founded by Bill Gates and Paul Allen."
tokens = word_tokenize(text)
tags = pos_tag(tokens)
tree = ne_chunk(tags)
# Convert tree to multiline string and print
print('\n'.join([' '.join([token for token, pos in subtree.leaves()]) for subtree in tree if isinstance(subtree, Tree)]))
```

This snippet identifies named entities in the text, showcasing NLTK's utility for extracting specific information from sentences.

Stemming and Lemmatization

Stemming and lemmatization are processes for reducing words to their base or root form. While stemming crudely chops off word endings, lemmatization considers the context and converts the word to its meaningful base form.

Example of Stemming and Lemmatization:

```
from nltk.stem import PorterStemmer, WordNetLemmatizer
from nltk.tokenize import word_tokenize
nltk.download('wordnet')
nltk.download('omw-1.4')
text = "The boys' cars are different colors."
tokens = word_tokenize(text)
stemmer = PorterStemmer()
lemmatizer = WordNetLemmatizer()
stems = [stemmer.stem(token) for token in tokens]
lemmas = [lemmatizer.lemmatize(token) for token in tokens]
print("Stemmed:", stems)
```

```
print("Lemmatized:", lemmas)
```

This demonstrates reducing words to their stems and lemmas, highlighting how NLTK supports both processes to normalize text.

NLTK offers a comprehensive toolkit for a wide range of NLP tasks, making it a staple in the NLP community for education, research, and application development. Its extensive collection of resources, straightforward API, and thorough documentation make it accessible to beginners while still being robust enough for complex NLP projects. Through examples of tokenization, POS tagging, NER, and more, we've seen how NLTK facilitates essential NLP processes, reinforcing its position as a fundamental library in the Python NLP ecosystem.

spaCy:

spaCy is a modern, fast, and industrially oriented Natural Language Processing (NLP) library for Python. Known for its efficiency and ease of use, spaCy is designed for real-world, production-ready applications. It excels in tasks such as tokenization, part-of-speech (POS) tagging, named entity recognition (NER), dependency parsing, and more, providing a comprehensive suite for advanced NLP needs. Unlike NLTK, which is generally preferred for educational purposes and prototyping, spaCy focuses on offering optimal performance and scalability for large-scale applications.

Tokenization with spaCy

spaCy provides highly efficient tokenization, automatically handling nuances like word boundaries and punctuation, making it a powerful tool for text preprocessing.

Example of Tokenization:

```
import spacy
nlp = spacy.load("en_core_web_sm")
text = "spaCy is a favorite among developers for NLP tasks."
doc = nlp(text)
```

```
tokens = [token.text for token in doc]
print(tokens)
```

This snippet processes the text into tokens using spaCy's language model, demonstrating spaCy's straightforward approach to breaking down text into its constituent parts.

Part-of-Speech Tagging and Dependency Parsing

Beyond simple tokenization, spaCy can analyze and assign part-of-speech tags to each token and parse sentence dependencies, which is crucial for understanding sentence structure.

Example of POS Tagging and Dependency Parsing:

```
for token in doc:
print(token.text, token.pos_, token.dep_, token.head.text)
```

This code iterates over each token in the document, printing out the text, its part-of-speech tag, dependency relation, and the syntactic head, showcasing spaCy's capability to provide detailed linguistic annotations.

Named Entity Recognition (NER)

spaCy includes a highly accurate named entity recognition component capable of identifying entities and classifying them into predefined categories such as PERSON, ORG, and GPE.

Example of NER:

```
for ent in doc.ents:
print(ent.text, ent.label_)
```

This extracts named entities from the text, along with their labels, leveraging spaCy's pre-trained NER model to identify and classify entities within the document.

Word Vectors and Semantic Similarity

One of spaCy's advanced features is its support for word vectors, enabling the computation of semantic similarity between words, text spans, and documents. spaCy models can include pre-trained word vectors from sources like GloVe.

Example of Semantic Similarity:

```
token1 = nlp("king")
```

```
token2 = nlp("queen")
print(token1.similarity(token2))
```

This computes the semantic similarity between "king" and "queen", demonstrating spaCy's ability to capture and compare the semantic meaning of words based on their vector representations.

Custom Pipeline Components and Extensions

spaCy allows for the customization and extension of its processing pipeline, enabling the integration of custom components and attributes tailored to specific NLP tasks.

Example of a Custom Pipeline Component:

```
def custom_component(doc):
# Custom processing and annotation
doc._.custom_attribute = "Custom Value"
return doc
# Add the component to the pipeline
nlp.add_pipe(custom_component, last=True)
```

This adds a custom processing component to spaCy's pipeline, illustrating the library's flexibility and adaptability to cater to specialized NLP requirements.

spaCy stands out in the Python NLP landscape for its performance, ease of use, and comprehensiveness, addressing a wide spectrum of NLP tasks from basic tokenization to complex entity recognition and linguistic analysis. Its design for real-world applications, support for multiple languages, and ability to integrate custom components make it a robust choice for developers and researchers aiming to deploy production-ready NLP solutions. Through the practical examples provided, we've showcased spaCy's capabilities, affirming its position as a leading NLP library in Python.

Transformers (Hugging Face):

The Transformers library by Hugging Face represents a significant advancement in Natural Language Processing (NLP) by providing access to state-of-the-art pre-trained models like BERT, GPT, RoBERTa, and T5. These transformer models have revolutionized the field with their remarkable performance across a wide range of NLP tasks, including text classification, named entity recognition, sentiment analysis, and machine translation. Python, being at the forefront of NLP research and application development, is the primary programming language for the Transformers library, facilitating ease of use, flexibility, and rapid prototyping.

Installation and Setup

To use the Transformers library, you first need to install it along with the torch or tensorflow backend, depending on your preference:

```
pip install transformers
```

Text Classification with BERT

Text classification is a fundamental NLP task, and BERT (Bi-directional Encoder Representations from Transformers) has set new standards for its performance. The Transformers library simplifies using BERT for text classification.

Example of Text Classification:

```
from transformers import pipeline
# Load a pre-trained model and tokenizer
classifier = pipeline('sentiment-analysis', model="bert-base-uncased")
# Classify text
result = classifier("Transformers library by Hugging Face makes NLP easy!")
print(result)
```

This example demonstrates using a pre-trained BERT model for sentiment analysis, showcasing the simplicity of performing complex NLP tasks with the Transformers library.

Named Entity Recognition (NER) with BERT

Named Entity Recognition (NER) is another area where

transformer models excel. The Transformers library provides an intuitive interface for using these models for NER.

Example of NER:

```
from transformers import pipeline
# Load a NER pipeline
ner_pipeline = pipeline("ner", model="dbmdz/bert-large-cased-finetuned-conll03-english")
# Perform NER on text
result = ner_pipeline("Hugging Face's Transformers library drastically simplifies NLP tasks.")
print(result)
```

This uses a BERT model fine-tuned on the CoNLL-03 dataset for NER, identifying entities within the text along with their categories.

Machine Translation with T5

T5 (Text-to-Text Transfer Transformer) is a versatile model capable of handling multiple NLP tasks, including machine translation, by framing NLP tasks as a text-to-text problem.

Example of Machine Translation:

```
from transformers import pipeline
# Load a translation pipeline
translator = pipeline("translation_en_to_de", model="t5-base")
# Translate text from English to German
translation = translator("Transformers library simplifies machine learning tasks.", max_length=40)
print(translation[0]['translation_text'])
```

This showcases T5's ability to perform machine translation, translating an English sentence into German with just a few lines of code.

Text Generation with GPT

Generative Pre-trained Transformer (GPT) models are designed for a wide range of generative tasks, including text generation. The Transformers library allows for easy utilization of GPT models for creating coherent and contextually relevant text.

Example of Text Generation:

```
from transformers import GPT2LMHeadModel, GPT2Tokenizer
tokenizer = GPT2Tokenizer.from_pretrained('gpt2')
model = GPT2LMHeadModel.from_pretrained('gpt2')
# Encode context and generate text
input_ids = tokenizer.encode('Python programming is', return_tensors='pt')
output = model.generate(input_ids, max_length=50, num_beams=5, early_stopping=True)
print(tokenizer.decode(output[0], skip_special_tokens=True))
```

This leverages GPT-2 for generating text that follows the given context, illustrating the power of transformer models in generating human-like text.

The Transformers library by Hugging Face has made cutting-edge NLP models and methods accessible to a broad audience, significantly lowering the barrier to entry for working with complex NLP tasks. Through its comprehensive suite of pre-trained models and task-specific pipelines, the library offers a versatile and powerful toolkit for NLP applications. The examples provided underscore the library's ease of use and flexibility, enabling developers and researchers to harness the capabilities of transformer models effectively within their Python-based NLP projects.

5. **Applications of NLP:**

Chatbots and Virtual Assistants:

Natural Language Processing (NLP) has been pivotal in revolutionizing how we interact with technology, with chatbots and virtual assistants emerging as significant applications. These AI-driven interfaces understand, interpret, and respond to human language in a way that mimics human conversation, enabling seamless interaction between humans and machines. Python, with its extensive NLP libraries and frameworks, stands at the forefront of developing these sophisticated systems.

Understanding User Intent

At the heart of chatbots and virtual assistants is the capability to comprehend user intent. This involves classifying the user's input into predefined categories (intents) and extracting relevant entities (slots). Libraries like spaCy and NLTK are instrumental in this process.

Example of Intent Classification and Entity Recognition:

```python
import spacy
nlp = spacy.load("en_core_web_sm")
user_input = "Book a flight to New York tomorrow morning."
doc = nlp(user_input)
# Intent classification (simplified for demonstration)
if "book" in user_input and "flight" in user_input:
intent = "book_flight"
else:
intent = "unknown"
# Entity recognition
entities = [(ent.text, ent.label_) for ent in doc.ents]
print("Intent:", intent)
print("Entities:", entities)
```

This example uses spaCy for entity recognition, aiding in identifying the 'New York' and 'tomorrow morning' entities as location and time, respectively. The intent is simplified to demonstrate the concept but, in practice, might use machine learning models trained on various user inputs.

Dialog Management

Dialog management involves determining the appropriate response based on the user's intent and entities. This can be achieved through rule-based systems for simple bots or more advanced machine learning models for complex dialogs.

Example of Dialog Management:

```
# Assuming the intent and entities were identified as above
def handle_book_flight(intent, entities):
location = next((e for e in entities if e[1] == "GPE"), ("Unknown",))[0]
    time = next((e for e in entities if e[1] == "DATE"), ("Unknown",))[0]
    return f"Booking flight to {location} for {time}."
    if intent == "book_flight":
    response = handle_book_flight(intent, entities)
    else:
    response = "I'm not sure how to help with that."
    print(response)
```

This rule-based dialog manager generates a response based on the identified intent and entities, simulating a basic level of conversational logic.

Utilizing Pre-trained Models for Natural Language Understanding

With the advent of transformer models like BERT and GPT from Hugging Face's Transformers library, understanding natural language has become more nuanced and contextually aware.

Example of Using Transformers for Enhanced Language Understanding:

```
from transformers import pipeline
nlp = pipeline("fill-mask", model="bert-base-uncased")
user_input = "Book a flight to [MASK] tomorrow morning."
predictions = nlp(user_input)
for pred in predictions:
print(pred)
```

Though not a direct application in chatbot development, this example demonstrates how transformer models can predict missing information or understand context, which can be integrated into more advanced systems for understanding nuances in user input.

Continuous Learning from Interactions

Advanced chatbots and virtual assistants improve over time by learning from user interactions. This can involve retraining models on new data or adjusting responses based on user feedback.

Example of Feedback Loop for Learning:

Simplified feedback loop

user_feedback = "The flight booking was incorrect."

new_training_data = [(user_input, user_feedback)]

Process and add the new training data to retrain the model

This step would involve NLP pipelines to preprocess and update the model

This concept illustrates incorporating user feedback into training data, which can refine and improve the bot's accuracy and relevance of responses.

Chatbots and virtual assistants exemplify the practical applications of NLP, bridging the gap between human communication and computational understanding. Python, through its rich NLP ecosystem, enables developers to build sophisticated systems that can parse intent, manage dialogs, and learn from interactions. From simple rule-based bots to advanced AI-driven assistants, NLP continues to redefine our interaction with technology, making digital services more accessible and intuitive.

Sentiment Analysis in Social Media:

Sentiment analysis in social media represents a significant application of Natural Language Processing (NLP), enabling businesses, researchers, and policymakers to gauge public opinion, monitor brand and product sentiment, and understand customer experiences on a large scale. With the exponential growth of user-generated content on platforms like Twitter, Facebook, and Reddit, sentiment analysis has become an invaluable tool for extracting insights from vast amounts of textual data. Python, with its extensive array of NLP libraries, stands as a prime technology for implementing sentiment analysis models.

Extracting Social Media Data

Before performing sentiment analysis, the first step involves collecting relevant social media data. Python libraries like Tweepy (for Twitter) facilitate this process by providing tools to interact with social media APIs.

Example of Extracting Tweets with Tweepy:

```
import tweepy
# Initialize API
auth = tweepy.OAuthHandler("CONSUMER_KEY", "CONSUMER_SECRET")
auth.set_access_token("ACCESS_TOKEN", "ACCESS_TOKEN_SECRET")
api = tweepy.API(auth)
# Fetch tweets related to Python programming
tweets = api.search(q="Python programming", count=100)
# Extract text from tweets
tweet_texts = [tweet.text for tweet in tweets]
```

This snippet demonstrates how to use Tweepy to fetch tweets related to Python programming, preparing the data for sentiment analysis.

Performing Sentiment Analysis

Once the data is collected, sentiment analysis can be performed using libraries like TextBlob or NLTK for straightforward approaches, or spaCy and Hugging Face's Transformers for more advanced models.

Example of Sentiment Analysis with TextBlob:

```
from textblob import TextBlob
# Sample tweet
tweet = "I love Python programming. It's amazing!"
# Perform sentiment analysis
blob = TextBlob(tweet)
sentiment = blob.sentiment.polarity # Ranges from -1 (negative) to 1 (positive)
print(f"Sentiment Polarity: {sentiment}")
```

This code evaluates the sentiment of a sample tweet, with TextBlob providing a polarity score that indicates the sentiment's positive or negative nature.

Example with Hugging Face's Transformers:

```
from transformers import pipeline
# Load sentiment analysis pipeline
classifier = pipeline("sentiment-analysis")
# Classify sentiment of tweets
results = classifier(tweet_texts)
for result, tweet in zip(results, tweet_texts):
print(f"Tweet: {tweet}, Sentiment: {result['label']}")
```

This uses a pre-trained model from Hugging Face's Transformers library to classify the sentiment of each tweet, showcasing the application of state-of-the-art models in social media sentiment analysis.

Analyzing Sentiment Trends

Sentiment analysis in social media can reveal trends over time, providing insights into public opinion dynamics, brand sentiment shifts, or reactions to events.

Example of Trend Analysis:

```
from collections import Counter
# Assuming 'results' contains sentiment analysis outcomes for multiple tweets over a period
sentiments = [result['label'] for result in results]
sentiment_counts = Counter(sentiments)
print(sentiment_counts)
```

This example aggregates sentiment analysis results to quantify positive and negative sentiments, facilitating trend analysis over the collected dataset.

Ethical Considerations and Challenges

Sentiment analysis in social media data presents ethical considerations, including privacy concerns and the potential for bias in models. It's crucial to handle data responsibly, respecting user privacy and being transparent about data use. Additionally, ensuring models are trained on diverse and representative datasets is vital to mitigate bias.

Sentiment analysis in social media is a powerful NLP application that transforms unstructured text into actionable insights, enabling a deeper understanding of public sentiment on a wide range of topics. Python, through its rich NLP ecosystem, offers the tools and libraries necessary to perform sentiment analysis, from data collection to advanced modeling. As social media continues to be a primary medium for public discourse, sentiment analysis will remain a key tool for gauging societal trends, opinions, and reactions, driving informed decision-making across various sectors.

Information Extraction:

Information Extraction (IE) is a pivotal application of Natural Language Processing (NLP) that focuses on automatically extracting structured information from unstructured and/or semi-structured text. This structured information often includes entities (names of people, organizations, locations), relationships between entities, and attributes related to entities (such as time, quantities, or descriptions). In the vast landscape of data, where a significant portion resides as text, information extraction enables the transformation of text into data that can be stored, queried, and analyzed efficiently. Python, with its extensive suite of NLP libraries, is exceptionally well-suited for developing information extraction systems.

Named Entity Recognition (NER)

Named Entity Recognition is a fundamental step in information extraction, identifying mentions of entities in text. Libraries such as spaCy and NLTK offer robust tools for NER.

Example with spaCy:

```
import spacy
nlp = spacy.load("en_core_web_sm")
text = "Apple Inc. announced the release of the iPhone 12 in Cupertino."
doc = nlp(text)
```

```
for ent in doc.ents:
print(ent.text, ent.label_)
```

This code uses spaCy to identify entities in a text, classifying them into categories such as organizations, products, and locations.

Relation Extraction

Relation Extraction aims to identify and classify semantic relationships between entities within a text, an essential task for building knowledge graphs from text data.

Example Using spaCy for Custom Relation Extraction:

```
# Assuming the entities have been identified as "Apple Inc." and "Cupertino"
apple = doc.ents[0]
cupertino = doc.ents[3]
# Extract sentence containing both entities
sentence = next(sent for sent in doc.sents if apple in sent and cupertino in sent)
# Define custom relation extraction
def extract_relation(sent):
# Simple pattern matching for demonstration purposes
if "announce" in sent.text or "release" in sent.text:
return "HEADQUARTERED_IN"
return "UNKNOWN"
relation = extract_relation(sentence)
print(f"Relation: {apple}, {relation}, {cupertino}")
```

This simplistic approach uses pattern matching to determine a relation between two identified entities based on the verbs or terms present in the sentence.

Coreference Resolution

Coreference resolution, identifying when two or more expressions in a text refer to the same entity, is crucial for fully understanding the context and for accurate information extraction.

Example with NeuralCoref and spaCy:

```
import spacy
```

```
import neuralcoref
nlp = spacy.load('en_core_web_sm')
neuralcoref.add_to_pipe(nlp)
text = "Apple was founded by Steve Jobs. The company creates innovative products."
doc = nlp(text)
# Resolve coreferences
resolved_text = doc._.coref_resolved
print(resolved_text)
```

This integrates NeuralCoref with spaCy, enhancing spaCy's NLP pipeline with the ability to resolve coreferences, making the text clearer for subsequent information extraction tasks.

Event Extraction

Event extraction involves identifying occurrences of specific types of events in text and the entities associated with those events, such as the time, location, and participants.

Custom Event Extraction with spaCy:

```
def extract_event(doc):
# Custom logic to extract "product release" events
for ent in doc.ents:
if ent.label_ == "PRODUCT" and "release" in ent.sent.text:
product = ent.text
# Extract additional event information...
return f"Product Release: {product}"
return "No event found."
doc = nlp("Apple announced the release of the iPhone 12.")
event_info = extract_event(doc)
print(event_info)
```

This custom function searches for product release events by looking for the "PRODUCT" entity type and relevant context around it.

Information extraction transforms unstructured text into structured data, paving the way for enhanced data analysis, knowledge discovery, and decision-making processes. Through the application of NLP techniques and Python libraries like spaCy, NLTK, and NeuralCoref, developers can implement sophisticated information extraction systems capable of identifying entities, extracting relationships, resolving coreferences, and detecting events. These capabilities are crucial across various domains, including business intelligence, legal document analysis, medical research, and beyond, showcasing the broad applicability and impact of information extraction in the era of data-driven decision-making.

Language Translation:

Language translation, a pivotal application of Natural Language Processing (NLP), epitomizes the blending of linguistic theory and computational technology to bridge human communication across language barriers. It involves converting text or speech from one language (source) to another (target) while preserving meaning and context. In the realm of Python programming, a suite of libraries and frameworks has been developed to facilitate and innovate in the field of machine translation, including but not limited to, statistical models, neural machine translation (NMT), and the revolutionary transformer models.

Statistical Machine Translation (SMT)

Statistical Machine Translation, though largely superseded by neural approaches, laid the groundwork for modern NMT systems. It relies on statistical models to translate text based on analyses of bilingual text corpora. While Python-specific examples for building SMT systems from scratch are extensive and beyond a brief overview, libraries such as NLTK provide interfaces for working with linguistic data that can be leveraged in SMT.

Neural Machine Translation (NMT) with seq2seq Models

NMT marked a significant advancement in translation quality, employing deep learning models to learn the mapping between source and target languages directly. The seq2seq (sequence-to-sequence) architecture, typically comprising encoder and decoder RNNs (Recurrent Neural Networks) or LSTMs (Long Short-Term Memory units), is a cornerstone of NMT.

Example with TensorFlow/Keras:

```
from tensorflow.keras.models import Model
from tensorflow.keras.layers import Input, LSTM, Dense
# This is a simplified version of constructing a seq2seq model for illustrative purposes.
# Define an input sequence and process it.
encoder_inputs = Input(shape=(None, num_encoder_tokens))
encoder = LSTM(latent_dim, return_state=True)
encoder_outputs, state_h, state_c = encoder(encoder_inputs)
# Discard `encoder_outputs` and only keep the states.
encoder_states = [state_h, state_c]
# Set up the decoder, using `encoder_states` as initial state.
decoder_inputs = Input(shape=(None, num_decoder_tokens))
decoder_lstm = LSTM(latent_dim, return_sequences=True, return_state=True)
decoder_outputs, _, _ = decoder_lstm(decoder_inputs, initial_state=encoder_states)
decoder_dense = Dense(num_decoder_tokens, activation='softmax')
decoder_outputs = decoder_dense(decoder_outputs)
# Define the model
model = Model([encoder_inputs, decoder_inputs], decoder_outputs)
# Model training and inference code would follow...
```

This snippet outlines a basic seq2seq model architecture, showcasing the structure but omitting detailed training and inference steps, which would typically involve significant additional code for data preprocessing, model training, and subsequent translation.

Transformers for State-of-the-Art Translation

Transformers, introduced by Vaswani et al. in "Attention is All You Need", have revolutionized NMT with their ability to handle long-range dependencies and parallelize training efficiently. The Hugging Face's Transformers library provides access to pre-trained transformer models like BERT and GPT, which can be fine-tuned for specific translation tasks.

Example with Hugging Face's Transformers:

```
from transformers import pipeline
# Load a pre-trained translation pipeline
translator = pipeline("translation_en_to_fr", model="t5-base")
# Translate text from English to French
translation = translator("Python is an excellent programming language for data analysis.", max_length=40)
print(translation[0]['translation_text'])
```

This example employs a pre-trained T5 model to translate an English sentence into French, demonstrating the ease of leveraging transformer models for language translation with minimal code.

Language Translation Evaluation

Evaluating the quality of translations remains an essential aspect of machine translation research and application. BLEU (Bilingual Evaluation Understudy) scores are commonly used to quantify the similarity between machine-generated translations and one or more reference translations, providing a metric for translation quality.

Language translation applications stand as a testament to the progress and potential of NLP in fostering global communication and understanding. Python's NLP ecosystem, including seq2seq models, transformer models from the Hugging Face's Transformers library, and other tools, offers a robust platform for developing and deploying machine translation systems. These technologies not only enable accurate and context-aware translations but also continue to push the boundaries of what's possible in breaking down language barriers through computational linguistics and artificial intelligence.

Text Summarization:

Text summarization is an essential application of Natural Language Processing (NLP) aimed at distilling the most important information from a source text to produce a condensed version. This task is vital in managing the overwhelming amount of textual data generated daily, enabling users to quickly grasp the essence of documents, articles, or reports. Python, with its rich NLP ecosystem, provides powerful tools for implementing both extractive and abstractive text summarization methods.

Extractive Text Summarization

Extractive summarization involves selecting significant sentences or fragments directly from the text and concatenating them to form a summary. This approach maintains the original text's integrity and is often easier to implement than abstractive summarization.

Example with Gensim:

Gensim is a Python library that offers simple and efficient tools for unsupervised semantic modeling. It includes functionalities for extractive summarization.

```python
from gensim.summarization import summarize

text = """
Python is an interpreted, high-level, general-purpose programming language. Created by Guido van Rossum and first released in 1991, Python's design philosophy emphasizes code readability with its notable use of significant whitespace. Its language constructs and object-oriented approach aim to help programmers write clear, logical code for small and large-scale projects.
"""

summary = summarize(text, word_count=50)
print(summary)
```

This code snippet demonstrates using Gensim to perform extractive summarization by selecting key sentences from the text until the specified word count is reached.

Abstractive Text Summarization

Abstractive summarization aims to generate a new, shorter text that conveys the most critical information from the original text, potentially rephrasing or using new expressions. This method mimics human summarization capabilities more closely.

Example with Hugging Face's Transformers:

The Transformers library by Hugging Face provides access to state-of-the-art models like BERT, GPT-2, and T5, which can be fine-tuned for abstractive text summarization tasks.

```python
from transformers import pipeline
# Load a pre-trained summarization pipeline
summarizer = pipeline("summarization", model="t5-small")
text = """
Python is an interpreted, high-level, general-purpose programming language. Created by Guido van Rossum and first released in 1991, Python's design philosophy emphasizes code readability with its notable use of significant whitespace. Its language constructs and object-oriented approach aim to help programmers write clear, logical code for small and large-scale projects.
"""

summary = summarizer(text, max_length=45, min_length=25, do_sample=False)
print(summary[0]['summary_text'])
```

This example employs a pre-trained T5 model to generate an abstractive summary of the provided text, showcasing the ability of transformer models to understand and condense content effectively.

Evaluation of Summarization Quality

Evaluating the quality of generated summaries is crucial for text summarization applications. ROUGE (Recall-Oriented Understudy for Gisting Evaluation) is a common metric used to compare the overlap between the generated summary and reference summaries, assessing the summarization model's performance.

Text summarization serves as a crucial application in the field of NLP, aiding in the efficient consumption and understanding of large volumes of text. Python's NLP libraries, such as Gensim for extractive summarization and the Transformers library for abstractive summarization, offer robust and accessible tools for developing summarization models. These technologies empower developers to create systems that can automatically generate concise and informative summaries, enhancing accessibility to information across various domains.

Conclusion:

Natural Language Processing (NLP) with Python has seen tremendous growth and advancement, enabling a wide range of applications across various industries. By leveraging powerful libraries and techniques, developers can analyze, understand, and generate human language text with ease. Understanding the principles, common tasks, and popular libraries in NLP is essential for effectively applying NLP techniques to real-world problems and building intelligent language-based applications.

Introduction To NLP And Its Applications:

Natural Language Processing (NLP) is a field of artificial intelligence that focuses on the interaction between computers and human languages. With the availability of robust libraries in Python such as NLTK, spaCy, and Transformers, NLP tasks have become more accessible and efficient to implement. This section provides a comprehensive overview of NLP and its applications, along with examples to illustrate its usage:

1. **Understanding Natural Language Processing (NLP):**

- NLP involves the development of algorithms and techniques to enable computers to understand, interpret, and generate human languages.
- It encompasses a wide range of tasks, including text processing, sentiment analysis, named entity recognition, machine translation, and text generation.

2. Applications of NLP:

1. Text Processing:

- NLP techniques are used to preprocess and clean text data by tokenizing, removing stop words, and performing stemming or lemmatization.
- Example: Tokenizing a sentence into words or phrases.

b. Sentiment Analysis:

- Sentiment analysis aims to determine the sentiment expressed in a piece of text, such as positive, negative, or neutral.
- Example: Analyzing customer reviews to determine overall sentiment towards a product.

c. Named Entity Recognition (NER):

- NER involves identifying and classifying named entities in text, such as person names, locations, organizations, and dates.
- Example: Extracting names of people, organizations, and locations from news articles.

d. Machine Translation:

- NLP techniques are used for translating text from one language to another, enabling cross-lingual communication.
- Example: Translating English text into French or vice versa.

e. Text Summarization:

- Text summarization involves condensing long documents or articles into shorter, more concise summaries while preserving key information.
- Example: Generating a summary of a research paper or news article.

3. Examples of NLP Tasks with Python:

1. **Tokenization with NLTK:**

   from nltk.tokenize import word_tokenize

   text = "Natural Language Processing is fascinating!"

   tokens = word_tokenize(text)

   print(tokens)

2. **Sentiment Analysis with spaCy:**

   import spacy

   from spacytextblob import TextBlob

   nlp = spacy.load('en_core_web_sm')

   text = "I love NLP and Python!"

   doc = nlp(text)

   print(doc._.polarity)

3. **Named Entity Recognition (NER) with Transformers:**

from transformers import pipeline

nlp = pipeline("ner")

text = "Apple Inc. is headquartered in Cupertino, California."

entities = nlp(text)

print(entities)

4. Real-world Applications of NLP:

1. **Chatbots and Virtual Assistants:**

- NLP techniques are used to build conversational agents capable of understanding and responding to human queries.
- Example: Virtual assistants like Siri, Alexa, and Google Assistant.

b. Social Media Monitoring:

- NLP is applied to analyze sentiment and extract insights from social media posts, tweets, and comments.

- Example: Analyzing Twitter data to understand public opinion on a particular topic.

c. Customer Feedback Analysis:

- NLP techniques are used to analyze customer reviews, feedback, and surveys to identify trends and patterns.
- Example: Analyzing product reviews on e-commerce platforms to understand customer satisfaction.

Natural Language Processing (NLP) with Python enables developers to build sophisticated applications capable of understanding, analyzing, and generating human language text. By leveraging powerful libraries and techniques, NLP can be applied to various real-world scenarios, including sentiment analysis, named entity recognition, machine translation, and text summarization. Understanding the fundamentals of NLP and its applications is essential for building intelligent language-based applications and systems.

Working With Text Data:

In Natural Language Processing (NLP), text data preprocessing is a crucial step to prepare raw text for analysis and modeling. This section explores the fundamental techniques of tokenization, stemming, and lemmatization, which are commonly used for text data preprocessing in Python.

1. **Tokenization:**

   Tokenization is the process of breaking down text into smaller units, such as words, phrases, or symbols. These smaller units are called tokens, and tokenization helps in extracting meaningful information from text data.

   Example using NLTK:

```python
from nltk.tokenize import word_tokenize
text = "Natural Language Processing is fascinating!"
tokens = word_tokenize(text)
print(tokens)
```

Output:

['Natural', 'Language', 'Processing', 'is', 'fascinating', '!']

2. **Stemming:**

Stemming is the process of reducing words to their root or base form, called the stem. It helps in reducing inflectional forms and derivationally related forms of words to their common base.

Example using NLTK:

```python
from nltk.stem import PorterStemmer
stemmer = PorterStemmer()
words = ["running", "runs", "ran"]
stemmed_words = [stemmer.stem(word) for word in words]
print(stemmed_words)
```

Output:

['run', 'run', 'ran']

3. **Lemmatization:**

Lemmatization is the process of reducing words to their base or dictionary form, called the lemma. Unlike stemming, lemmatization considers the context of the word to determine its lemma, resulting in more accurate results.

Example using NLTK:

```python
from nltk.stem import WordNetLemmatizer
lemmatizer = WordNetLemmatizer()
words = ["running", "runs", "ran"]
lemmatized_words = [lemmatizer.lemmatize(word) for word in words]
print(lemmatized_words)
```

Output:

['running', 'run', 'ran']

4. **Comparison:**

- **Tokenization:** Breaks text into individual tokens, such as words or phrases.
- **Stemming:** Reduces words to their root form, which may not always be a valid word.
- **Lemmatization:** Reduces words to their base form, considering the context and producing valid words.

5. Use Cases:

- **Tokenization:** Used for text analysis, language modeling, and feature extraction.
- **Stemming:** Often used in information retrieval, search engines, and text classification tasks.
- **Lemmatization:** Preferred in applications requiring accurate word representations, such as machine translation, sentiment analysis, and named entity recognition.

Tokenization, stemming, and lemmatization are essential text preprocessing techniques in NLP. While tokenization breaks text into meaningful units, stemming and lemmatization reduce words to their base forms, facilitating further analysis and understanding of text data. Understanding when to use each technique and how they impact downstream tasks is crucial for effective text data preprocessing and NLP applications in Python.

Building NLP Models:

Natural Language Processing (NLP) models can be built using various Python libraries, including NLTK (Natural Language Toolkit) and spaCy. These libraries provide a wide range of tools and functionalities to perform text processing, feature extraction, and model training. This section delves into building NLP models using NLTK and spaCy, along with examples to illustrate their usage.

1. **NLTK (Natural Language Toolkit):**

   NLTK is a popular library for NLP tasks, offering a comprehensive suite of tools and resources for text processing, tokenization, stemming, lemmatization, part-of-speech tagging, named entity recognition, and more.

   Example: Building a Sentiment Analysis Model with NLTK:

```python
import nltk
from nltk.corpus import movie_reviews
from nltk.tokenize import word_tokenize
from nltk.classify import NaiveBayesClassifier
from nltk.classify.util import accuracy
# Prepare data
documents = [(list(movie_reviews.words(fileid)), category)
for category in movie_reviews.categories()
for fileid in movie_reviews.fileids(category)]
random.shuffle(documents)
# Feature extraction
all_words = nltk.FreqDist(word.lower() for word in movie_reviews.words())
word_features = list(all_words.keys())[:2000]
def document_features(document):
document_words = set(document)
features = {}
for word in word_features:
features['contains({})'.format(word)]  =  (word in document_words)
return features
# Train/test split
featuresets = [(document_features(d), c) for (d, c) in documents]
train_set, test_set = featuresets[:1900], featuresets[1900:]
# Train the classifier
classifier = NaiveBayesClassifier.train(train_set)
```

```python
# Evaluate the classifier
print('Accuracy:', accuracy(classifier, test_set))
```

2. **spaCy:**

spaCy is another powerful library for NLP tasks, known for its efficiency, accuracy, and ease of use. It provides pre-trained models for various languages and tasks, such as tokenization, part-of-speech tagging, dependency parsing, named entity recognition, and text classification.

Example: Named Entity Recognition (NER) with spaCy:

```python
import spacy
# Load pre-trained English model
nlp = spacy.load('en_core_web_sm')
# Process text
text = "Apple is looking to buy a startup for $1 billion"
doc = nlp(text)
# Extract named entities
for ent in doc.ents:
print(ent.text, ent.label_)
```

Output:

```
Apple ORG
$1 billion MONEY
```

3. **Comparison:**

- **NLTK:** Offers a wide range of tools and resources for NLP tasks, suitable for educational purposes and research.
- **spaCy:** Provides optimized, production-ready models and pipelines, ideal for building scalable and efficient NLP applications.

4. **Use Cases:**

- **NLTK:** Often used for educational purposes, rapid prototyping, and experimenting with NLP algorithms and techniques.

- **spaCy:** Preferred for building production-grade NLP applications, such as chatbots, sentiment analysis systems, and information extraction pipelines.

Conclusion:

NLTK and spaCy are two powerful libraries for building NLP models in Python. While NLTK offers a comprehensive suite of tools for text processing and analysis, spaCy provides optimized models and pipelines for production-grade NLP applications. Understanding the strengths and limitations of each library is essential for choosing the right tool for your NLP project.

Chapter 8: Reinforcement Learning

Reinforcement Learning (RL) is a machine learning paradigm where an agent learns to make decisions by interacting with an environment in order to maximize cumulative rewards. Unlike supervised learning, where the model is trained on labeled data, or unsupervised learning, where the model learns patterns from unlabeled data, RL is about learning through trial and error.

1. **Core Components of Reinforcement Learning:**

1. **Agent:** The learner or decision-maker that interacts with the environment.

2. **Environment:** The external system with which the agent interacts.

3. **Actions:** The set of possible decisions or choices that the agent can take.

4. **State:** A representation of the current situation or configuration of the environment.

5. **Rewards:** Numeric signals that the agent receives as feedback for its actions. The goal of the agent is to maximize cumulative rewards over time.

2. Reinforcement Learning Process:

1. **Exploration vs. Exploitation:** The agent must balance between exploring new actions to discover better strategies and exploiting known actions to maximize immediate rewards.
2. **Policy:** A strategy or mapping from states to actions that guides the agent's behavior.
3. **Value Function:** An estimate of the expected cumulative rewards obtained from following a particular policy.
4. **Q-Value (Action-Value) Function:** The expected cumulative rewards obtained by taking a particular action in a particular state and then following a policy thereafter.

3. Reinforcement Learning Algorithms:

1. **Q-Learning:** An off-policy RL algorithm that learns the optimal action-value function by iteratively updating Q-values based on observed rewards.
2. **Deep Q-Networks (DQN):** A variant of Q-learning that uses a deep neural network to approximate the Q-value function, enabling RL in high-dimensional state spaces.
3. **Policy Gradient Methods:** RL algorithms that directly optimize the policy by gradient descent, such as REINFORCE and Actor-Critic methods.

4. Example: Q-Learning for Gridworld Navigation:

Consider a gridworld environment where an agent needs to navigate from a start state to a goal state while avoiding obstacles.

```
import numpy as np
# Initialize Q-values
Q = np.zeros((num_states, num_actions))
# Q-Learning algorithm
for episode in range(num_episodes):
state = env.reset()
done = False
```

```
while not done:
action = np.argmax(Q[state])
next_state, reward, done, _ = env.step(action)
Q[state, action] += alpha * (reward + gamma * np.max(Q[next_state]) - Q[state, action])
state = next_state
```

5. Applications of Reinforcement Learning:

1. **Game Playing:** RL has achieved remarkable success in mastering complex games like Go, Chess, and video games.
2. **Robotics:** RL is used to train robotic agents for tasks like manipulation, navigation, and locomotion.
3. **Autonomous Vehicles:** RL techniques are employed in training self-driving cars to navigate safely and efficiently.
4. **Finance:** RL algorithms are used in algorithmic trading, portfolio optimization, and risk management.

6. Challenges in Reinforcement Learning:

1. **Exploration-Exploitation Tradeoff:** Finding the right balance between exploring new actions and exploiting known actions is a key challenge.
2. **Reward Design:** Designing reward functions that effectively guide the agent towards desired behavior can be challenging.
3. **Sample Efficiency:** RL algorithms often require large amounts of data or samples to learn effective policies, which can be impractical in real-world applications.

Reinforcement Learning is a powerful framework for training intelligent agents to make decisions by interacting with their environments. By learning from trial and error, RL algorithms can achieve remarkable results in various domains, from game playing to robotics and finance.

Understanding the core concepts, algorithms, and challenges in RL is essential for effectively applying this paradigm to real-world problems.

Introduction To Reinforcement Learning:

Reinforcement Learning (RL) is a branch of machine learning concerned with how an agent learns to make decisions by interacting with an environment in order to achieve certain goals. Unlike supervised learning where data is labeled, or unsupervised learning where patterns are inferred from unlabeled data, RL involves learning through trial and error with feedback in the form of rewards or penalties.

1. **Core Components of Reinforcement Learning:**
   1. **Agent:** The decision-making entity that interacts with the environment.
   2. **Environment:** The external system with which the agent interacts. It is represented by a set of states, actions, and transition dynamics.
   3. **State:** A representation of the current situation or configuration of the environment. It provides the necessary information for the agent to make decisions.
   4. **Action:** The set of possible decisions or choices that the agent can take. Actions are chosen based on the current state of the environment.
   5. **Reward:** A numerical signal that the agent receives as feedback for its actions. It indicates the desirability of the state-action pair.

2. Exploration vs. Exploitation:

In RL, the agent faces the exploration-exploitation dilemma, where it must decide between exploring new actions to discover better strategies or exploiting known actions to maximize immediate rewards. Striking the right balance between exploration and exploitation is crucial for effective learning.

3. Markov Decision Processes (MDPs):

MDPs provide a mathematical framework for modeling sequential decision-making under uncertainty. They consist of states, actions, transition probabilities, and rewards. The Markov property assumes that the future state depends only on the current state and action, not the past history of states and actions.

4. Value Functions:

Value functions estimate the expected cumulative rewards obtained from following a particular policy. They help the agent evaluate the desirability of states or state-action pairs.

- **State Value Function (V):** Estimates the expected cumulative rewards obtained from a particular state under a given policy.
- **Action Value Function (Q):** Estimates the expected cumulative rewards obtained by taking a particular action in a particular state and then following a policy thereafter.

5. Policy:

A policy is a mapping from states to actions that guides the agent's behavior. It defines the strategy or decision-making mechanism of the agent. Policies can be deterministic or stochastic.

6. Example: Gridworld Navigation:

Consider a gridworld environment where an agent needs to navigate from a start state to a goal state while avoiding obstacles. The agent receives a reward of +1 upon reaching the goal state and -1 upon colliding with an obstacle.

The agent's goal is to learn a policy that maximizes cumulative rewards over time, leading to efficient navigation through the gridworld.

7. Applications of Reinforcement Learning:

- **Game Playing:** RL has achieved remarkable success in mastering complex games like Go, Chess, and video games.

- **Robotics:** RL is used to train robotic agents for tasks like manipulation, navigation, and locomotion.
- **Autonomous Vehicles:** RL techniques are employed in training self-driving cars to navigate safely and efficiently.
- **Finance:** RL algorithms are used in algorithmic trading, portfolio optimization, and risk management.

Reinforcement Learning is a powerful framework for training intelligent agents to make decisions by interacting with their environments. By learning through trial and error with feedback in the form of rewards, RL algorithms can achieve remarkable results in various domains. Understanding the core concepts of RL, including agents, environments, states, actions, rewards, and policies, is essential for effectively applying this paradigm to real-world problems.

Learning Algorithms in Python:

Implementing reinforcement learning (RL) algorithms in Python involves translating the theoretical concepts into code to create agents that interact with environments, learn from experience, and improve their decision-making over time. This section explores the process of implementing RL algorithms, along with examples to illustrate their usage.

1. **Environment Setup:**

   Before implementing RL algorithms, it's essential to define the environment in which the agent will operate. The environment consists of states, actions, transition dynamics, and reward signals. Implementing the environment involves creating classes or functions to represent these components and define their interactions.

   Example: Gridworld Environment

   class Gridworld:

```python
def __init__(self, size):
self.size = size
self.state = (0, 0)
self.goal = (size-1, size-1)
self.obstacles = [(1, 1), (2, 2)] # Define obstacle locations
def reset(self):
self.state = (0, 0)
def step(self, action):
# Implement state transitions based on actions
# Update agent's state and return reward
```

2. **Agent Implementation:**

Once the environment is set up, the next step is to implement the RL agent that interacts with the environment, learns from experience, and makes decisions to maximize cumulative rewards. The agent typically has a policy that guides its actions and learns from feedback in the form of rewards.

Example: Q-Learning Agent

```python
import numpy as np
class QLearningAgent:
def __init__(self, num_states, num_actions, alpha, gamma, epsilon):
self.Q = np.zeros((num_states, num_actions))
self.alpha = alpha
self.gamma = gamma
self.epsilon = epsilon
def choose_action(self, state):
if np.random.rand() < self.epsilon:
return np.random.randint(num_actions)
else:
return np.argmax(self.Q[state])
def update_Q(self, state, action, reward, next_state):
self.Q[state, action] += self.alpha * (reward + self.gamma * np.max(self.Q[next_state]) - self.Q[state, action])
def train(self, env, num_episodes):
```

```
for episode in range(num_episodes):
state = env.reset()
done = False
while not done:
action = self.choose_action(state)
next_state, reward, done, _ = env.step(action)
self.update_Q(state, action, reward, next_state)
state = next_state
```

3. **Training the Agent:**

   Once the agent and environment are implemented, the agent needs to be trained using RL algorithms. During training, the agent interacts with the environment, collects experience, and updates its policy or value function based on observed rewards.

   Example: Training the Q-Learning Agent

```
env = Gridworld(size=5)
agent = QLearningAgent(num_states=env.size**2, num_actions=4, alpha=0.1, gamma=0.9, epsilon=0.1)
agent.train(env, num_episodes=1000)
```

4. **Evaluation and Testing:**

   After training, the agent's performance needs to be evaluated to assess its effectiveness in solving the task. This involves testing the agent in the environment and measuring its performance metrics such as cumulative rewards, success rate, or convergence speed.

   Example: Evaluating the Q-Learning Agent

```
def evaluate_agent(agent, env, num_episodes):
total_rewards = []
for _ in range(num_episodes):
state = env.reset()
episode_reward = 0
done = False
while not done:
action = agent.choose_action(state)
```

```
next_state, reward, done, _ = env.step(action)
episode_reward += reward
state = next_state
total_rewards.append(episode_reward)
avg_reward = np.mean(total_rewards)
print("Average Reward:", avg_reward)
```

5. **Example RL Algorithms:**

- **Q-Learning**
- **Deep Q-Networks (DQN)**
- **Policy Gradient Methods (e.g., REINFORCE)**
- **Actor-Critic Methods**

6. Libraries for RL Implementation:

- **OpenAI Gym:** Provides a collection of RL environments for testing and benchmarking algorithms.
- **Stable Baselines:** A set of high-quality implementations of RL algorithms built on top of OpenAI Gym.

Implementing reinforcement learning algorithms in Python involves defining the environment, designing the agent, training the agent using RL algorithms, and evaluating its performance. By translating theoretical concepts into code, practitioners can develop RL agents capable of solving complex tasks and learning from experience.

Building Agents to Solve Simple Problems:

OpenAI Gym is a toolkit for developing and comparing reinforcement learning algorithms. It provides a wide range of environments, from simple grid worlds to complex video games, where agents can interact, learn, and improve their decision-making capabilities. This section explores the process of building agents to solve simple problems using OpenAI Gym, along with examples to illustrate their implementation.

1. Introduction to OpenAI Gym:

OpenAI Gym offers a collection of environments, each with a well-defined interface consisting of states, actions, rewards, and termination conditions. These environments serve as testbeds for evaluating and benchmarking reinforcement learning algorithms.

2. Building an Environment:

To build an agent, first, select an environment from OpenAI Gym or create a custom environment using Gym's interface. Define the states, actions, rewards, and transition dynamics of the environment.

Example: CartPole Environment

```
import gym
env = gym.make('CartPole-v1')
```

3. Interacting with the Environment:

The agent interacts with the environment by selecting actions and receiving observations (states) and rewards. The agent's goal is to learn a policy that maximizes cumulative rewards over time.

Example: Random Agent

```
env.reset()
done = False
total_reward = 0
while not done:
    action = env.action_space.sample() # Choose a random action
    next_state, reward, done, _ = env.step(action)
    total_reward += reward
```

4. Implementing RL Algorithms:

Choose a reinforcement learning algorithm to train the agent. Implement the algorithm, including exploration strategies, value function updates, and policy improvements, using the observations and rewards obtained from the environment.

Example: Q-Learning Agent

```
import numpy as np
```

```python
Q = np.zeros((env.observation_space.n, env.action_space.n))
alpha = 0.1 # Learning rate
gamma = 0.9 # Discount factor
epsilon = 0.1 # Exploration rate
state = env.reset()
done = False
while not done:
if np.random.rand() < epsilon:
action = env.action_space.sample() # Explore
else:
action = np.argmax(Q[state]) # Exploit
next_state, reward, done, _ = env.step(action)
Q[state, action] += alpha * (reward + gamma * np.max(Q[next_state]) - Q[state, action])
state = next_state
```

5. Evaluating Agent Performance:

After training, evaluate the agent's performance by testing it in the environment and measuring its performance metrics, such as average cumulative rewards, success rate, or convergence speed.

Example: Evaluating Q-Learning Agent

```python
total_rewards = []
for _ in range(num_episodes):
state = env.reset()
episode_reward = 0
done = False
while not done:
action = np.argmax(Q[state])
next_state, reward, done, _ = env.step(action)
episode_reward += reward
state = next_state
total_rewards.append(episode_reward)
avg_reward = np.mean(total_rewards)
print("Average Reward:", avg_reward)
```

6. Example Problems:

- **CartPole:** Balance a pole on a moving cart by applying left or right forces.
- **MountainCar:** Drive a car up a steep mountain by applying throttle and steering actions.
- **FrozenLake:** Navigate a frozen lake to reach the goal while avoiding holes.

7. Libraries for Reinforcement Learning:

- **Stable Baselines:** A set of high-quality implementations of RL algorithms built on top of OpenAI Gym.
- **RLlib:** An open-source library for scalable reinforcement learning algorithms.

Conclusion:

OpenAI Gym provides a convenient framework for developing and testing reinforcement learning algorithms. By building agents to solve simple problems using Gym environments, practitioners can gain insights into the RL process and explore the effectiveness of various algorithms in different scenarios.

Chapter 9: Case Studies and Projects

Case studies and projects are essential components of learning reinforcement learning (RL) as they provide practical applications of theoretical concepts, allowing practitioners to gain hands-on experience and deepen their understanding of RL algorithms. This section explores the significance of case studies and projects in RL, along with examples to illustrate their implementation.

1. **Importance of Case Studies and Projects:**

1. **Real-world Application:** Case studies and projects enable practitioners to apply RL techniques to real-world problems, bridging the gap between theory and practice.

2. **Hands-on Experience:** Engaging in case studies and projects provides practical, hands-on experience in implementing RL algorithms, strengthening problem-solving skills and algorithmic understanding.

3. **Skill Development:** By working on projects, practitioners develop a wide range of skills, including data analysis, algorithm implementation, model evaluation, and result interpretation.

4. **Portfolio Building:** Completing projects allows practitioners to build a portfolio showcasing their expertise in RL, which can be beneficial for career advancement or academic pursuits.

2. Examples of Case Studies and Projects:

1. **CartPole Balancing with Q-Learning:** Implement Q-learning to train an agent to balance a pole on a cart in the CartPole environment. Experiment with different learning rates and exploration strategies to improve agent performance.
2. **Gridworld Navigation with Policy Gradient Methods:** Use policy gradient methods such as REINFORCE to train an agent to navigate a gridworld environment. Evaluate the agent's performance under different reward structures and policies.
3. **Autonomous Vehicle Navigation in Simulated City:** Develop an RL-based navigation system for an autonomous vehicle to navigate through a simulated city environment. Train the vehicle to follow traffic rules, avoid obstacles, and reach its destination efficiently.
4. **Stock Trading Strategy Optimization:** Design an RL-based trading strategy to optimize stock trading decisions. Train an agent to learn trading policies that maximize profits while minimizing risks using historical stock market data.

3. Project Implementation Process:

1. **Problem Definition:** Clearly define the problem statement, including the environment, objectives, constraints, and evaluation metrics.
2. **Data Collection and Preprocessing:** Gather relevant data if applicable, preprocess it, and format it for use in the RL algorithm.
3. **Algorithm Selection:** Choose an appropriate RL algorithm or combination of algorithms based on the problem requirements and characteristics.

4. **Model Training:** Train the RL agent using the selected algorithm(s), fine-tuning hyperparameters and conducting experiments to optimize performance.

5. **Evaluation and Analysis:** Evaluate the trained model's performance using appropriate metrics, analyze results, and draw conclusions about the effectiveness of the approach.

6. **Documentation and Presentation:** Document the project process, results, and findings in a clear and concise manner. Present the project outcomes through reports, presentations, or online platforms.

4. Benefits of Completing Case Studies and Projects:

1. **Skill Enhancement:** Case studies and projects provide opportunities to enhance technical skills in RL algorithms, programming languages, and data analysis techniques.

2. **Portfolio Development:** Completing projects allows practitioners to build a portfolio showcasing their expertise and accomplishments, which can be shared with potential employers or collaborators.

3. **Problem-solving Abilities:** Working on projects challenges practitioners to apply creative problem-solving techniques to tackle complex RL problems, fostering critical thinking and innovation.

4. **Networking Opportunities:** Sharing project outcomes through online platforms, forums, or communities facilitates networking and collaboration with peers and experts in the RL community.

Case studies and projects are integral components of learning reinforcement learning, offering practitioners opportunities to apply theoretical knowledge to practical problems and develop essential skills. By engaging in projects, practitioners gain hands-on experience, deepen their understanding of RL algorithms, and build a portfolio of successful implementations, setting the stage for continued growth and success in the field.

Real-World Case Studies:

Case studies and projects serve as pivotal tools for understanding the practical applications of artificial intelligence (AI) in Python. By delving into real-world scenarios and implementing AI solutions, practitioners can gain valuable insights into how AI technologies can be leveraged to solve complex problems across various domains. Below, we explore the significance of case studies and projects in AI, along with examples illustrating their real-world applications.

1. **Significance of Real-world Case Studies and Projects:**

   1. **Practical Understanding:** Real-world case studies and projects provide practitioners with a practical understanding of how AI techniques are applied to solve complex problems in diverse domains.

   2. **Hands-on Experience:** Engaging in projects offers hands-on experience in implementing AI algorithms, data preprocessing, model training, evaluation, and deployment.

   3. **Problem-solving Skills:** By tackling real-world challenges, practitioners hone their problem-solving skills, learning how to identify, formulate, and address complex problems using AI techniques.

   4. **Domain Expertise:** Case studies and projects allow practitioners to gain domain-specific knowledge by working on applications tailored to specific industries or sectors.

2. **Examples of Real-world Case Studies and Applications:**

   1. **Healthcare: Predicting Disease Outcomes**

- **Problem:** Develop an AI model to predict disease outcomes based on patient data such as medical history, genetic information, and lifestyle factors.
- **Implementation:** Utilize machine learning algorithms such as logistic regression, decision trees, or deep learning models to analyze patient data and predict disease progression, treatment response, or risk factors.

b. Finance: Fraud Detection

- **Problem:** Build an AI system to detect fraudulent transactions or activities in financial transactions.
- **Implementation:** Employ techniques such as anomaly detection, pattern recognition, or supervised learning algorithms to identify suspicious transactions and flag potential instances of fraud.

c. Retail: Personalized Recommendations

- **Problem:** Create a recommendation system to provide personalized product recommendations to customers based on their browsing history, purchase behavior, and preferences.
- **Implementation:** Develop collaborative filtering algorithms, content-based filtering, or hybrid recommendation systems to analyze customer data and deliver tailored product suggestions.

d. Transportation: Traffic Prediction and Optimization

- **Problem:** Develop an AI model to predict traffic patterns, congestion levels, and travel times to optimize route planning and traffic management.
- **Implementation:** Utilize time series forecasting techniques, reinforcement learning, or predictive analytics to analyze historical

traffic data and predict future traffic conditions, enabling efficient route planning and congestion mitigation.

3. Project Implementation Process:

1. **Problem Identification:** Clearly define the problem statement, objectives, and requirements based on real-world challenges in the chosen domain.
2. **Data Collection and Preprocessing:** Gather relevant data sources, clean and preprocess the data to remove noise, handle missing values, and prepare it for analysis.
3. **Algorithm Selection:** Choose appropriate AI algorithms and techniques based on the nature of the problem, available data, and desired outcomes.
4. **Model Training and Evaluation:** Train the AI model using the selected algorithms, validate its performance using suitable evaluation metrics, and fine-tune the model parameters as needed.
5. **Deployment and Integration:** Deploy the trained AI model into production environments, integrate it with existing systems or applications, and monitor its performance over time.

4. Benefits of Real-world Case Studies and Projects:

1. **Practical Learning:** Real-world case studies and projects provide practical learning experiences, allowing practitioners to apply theoretical knowledge to solve tangible problems.
2. **Skill Development:** Engaging in projects fosters skill development in AI algorithms, programming languages, data analysis, and problem-solving techniques.
3. **Domain Expertise:** Working on projects in specific domains enables practitioners to gain domain-specific knowledge and expertise, enhancing their credibility and value in those industries.

4. **Innovation and Creativity:** Case studies and projects encourage innovation and creativity by challenging practitioners to devise novel solutions to real-world challenges using AI techniques.

Real-world case studies and projects play a vital role in understanding the practical applications of AI in Python. By working on projects tailored to specific domains and applications, practitioners gain practical experience, develop essential skills, and contribute to solving complex problems across various industries. Through hands-on engagement with real-world challenges, practitioners can unlock the full potential of AI technologies and drive innovation in their respective fields.

Hands-On Projects to Reinforce Learning:

Hands-on projects are integral to reinforcing learning in any field, including artificial intelligence (AI). By actively engaging in projects, practitioners not only solidify their understanding of theoretical concepts but also gain practical experience in implementing AI techniques. This section explores the significance of hands-on projects in reinforcing AI learning, along with examples to illustrate their implementation.

1. **Importance of Hands-On Projects:**
1. **Application of Theory:** Hands-on projects allow practitioners to apply theoretical knowledge acquired through courses or textbooks to real-world scenarios, enhancing understanding and retention.
2. **Skill Development:** By working on projects, practitioners develop practical skills in data preprocessing, algorithm implementation, model evaluation, and result interpretation, which are essential for success in AI roles.

3. **Problem-Solving Practice:** Projects provide opportunities to tackle complex problems and develop effective problem-solving strategies, fostering creativity and innovation in AI applications.

4. **Portfolio Building:** Completed projects serve as tangible evidence of skills and accomplishments, enriching practitioners' portfolios and showcasing their capabilities to potential employers or collaborators.

2. Examples of Hands-On Projects:

1. **Image Classification with Convolutional Neural Networks (CNNs):**

   - **Problem:** Develop an AI model to classify images into predefined categories, such as identifying different types of animals or objects in images.
   - **Implementation:** Utilize CNN architectures such as VGG, ResNet, or MobileNet to train a model on labeled image datasets, achieving high accuracy in classifying images.

b. **Sentiment Analysis on Social Media Data:**

   - **Problem:** Analyze sentiment expressed in social media posts or comments to determine the overall sentiment (positive, negative, neutral) towards a specific topic or product.
   - **Implementation:** Apply natural language processing (NLP) techniques, including tokenization, word embedding, and recurrent neural networks (RNNs), to analyze textual data and classify sentiments.

c. **Predictive Maintenance in Manufacturing:**

- **Problem:** Develop a predictive maintenance system to anticipate equipment failures and schedule maintenance activities proactively, minimizing downtime and maintenance costs.
- **Implementation:** Employ machine learning algorithms such as random forests, support vector machines (SVM), or deep learning models to analyze sensor data and predict equipment failures.

d. Autonomous Drone Navigation:

- **Problem:** Design an autonomous navigation system for drones to navigate through indoor or outdoor environments, avoiding obstacles and reaching designated destinations safely.
- **Implementation:** Combine computer vision techniques for object detection and tracking with reinforcement learning algorithms for navigation policy learning in dynamic environments.

3. Project Implementation Process:

1. **Problem Definition:** Clearly define the problem statement, objectives, constraints, and evaluation metrics for the project.
2. **Data Collection and Preprocessing:** Gather relevant data sources, clean and preprocess the data to remove noise, handle missing values, and format it for use in AI models.
3. **Algorithm Selection and Model Design:** Choose appropriate AI algorithms and techniques based on the problem requirements, data characteristics, and desired outcomes. Design the architecture of AI models, considering factors such as model complexity, computational resources, and performance goals.
4. **Model Training and Evaluation:** Train the AI models using the selected algorithms, validate their performance using appropriate evaluation metrics, and fine-tune model parameters as needed to optimize performance.

5. **Deployment and Integration:** Deploy the trained AI models into production environments, integrate them with existing systems or applications, and monitor their performance in real-world settings.

4. Benefits of Hands-On Projects:

1. **Practical Learning:** Hands-on projects provide practical learning experiences, reinforcing theoretical concepts and enabling practitioners to apply AI techniques to real-world problems.
2. **Skill Development:** Engaging in projects fosters skill development in AI algorithms, programming languages, data analysis, and problem-solving techniques, enhancing practitioners' proficiency and expertise in AI.
3. **Creativity and Innovation:** Projects encourage creativity and innovation by challenging practitioners to devise novel solutions to complex problems, fostering exploration and experimentation in AI applications.
4. **Career Advancement:** Successful completion of hands-on projects demonstrates competence and proficiency in AI, enhancing practitioners' credibility and competitiveness in the job market or academic pursuits.

Conclusion:

Hands-on projects play a crucial role in reinforcing learning and mastering AI techniques. By actively engaging in projects, practitioners gain practical experience, develop essential skills, and contribute to solving real-world problems using AI technologies. Through hands-on exploration and experimentation, practitioners can unlock the full potential of AI and drive innovation in diverse domains and industries.

Chapter 10: Future of AI and Python

In recent years, Python has emerged as a dominant programming language in the field of artificial intelligence (AI), owing to its simplicity, flexibility, and extensive ecosystem of libraries and frameworks. As AI continues to evolve rapidly, Python is poised to play a pivotal role in shaping the future of this transformative technology. Below, we explore the future prospects of AI and Python, along with examples highlighting their potential impact across various domains.

1. **Advancements in AI Technology:**

1. **Deep Learning Breakthroughs:**

Deep learning, a subfield of AI, has witnessed significant advancements driven by innovations in neural network architectures, optimization algorithms, and hardware accelerators. Python frameworks such as TensorFlow and PyTorch have been instrumental in facilitating research and development in deep learning, leading to breakthroughs in computer vision, natural language processing, and reinforcement learning.

As we look ahead, the convergence of AI and Python is poised to drive significant advancements across various domains. Let's delve into the future prospects of AI technology and Python's role in facilitating these advancements, along with illustrative examples:

1. **Breakthroughs in Deep Learning:**

1. **Advanced Neural Network Architectures:** The future holds promise for more sophisticated neural network architectures, including attention mechanisms, transformers, and capsule networks. These architectures aim to improve model interpretability, handle complex data types more effectively, and achieve state-of-the-art performance in tasks such as natural language understanding, image recognition, and reinforcement learning.

2. **Automated Machine Learning (AutoML):** AutoML techniques leverage Python libraries such as scikit-learn and TensorFlow to automate the process of model selection, hyperparameter tuning, and feature engineering. In the future, AutoML systems will become more efficient and user-friendly, enabling non-experts to build high-performing AI models with minimal manual intervention.

Example: Google's AutoML platform enables users to train custom machine learning models for various tasks, including image classification, text classification, and structured data analysis, without requiring deep expertise in machine learning algorithms.

2. **Advancements in Natural Language Processing (NLP):**

1. **Transformative Language Models:** Recent advancements in transformer-based models, such as OpenAI's GPT (Generative Pre-trained Transformer) series and Google's BERT (Bidirectional Encoder Representations from Transformers), have revolutionized NLP tasks by enabling more context-aware, fluent, and coherent text generation and understanding.

2. **Multimodal AI:** The integration of language understanding with other modalities such as vision and audio will lead to the development of more comprehensive AI systems capable of understanding and generating content across multiple sensory domains.

Example: OpenAI's GPT-3 model demonstrates remarkable capabilities in natural language understanding and generation, showcasing the potential of large-scale transformer architectures for various NLP applications, including text completion, translation, and question answering.

3. Advancements in Computer Vision:

1. **Self-Supervised Learning:** Future advancements in self-supervised learning techniques will enable AI systems to learn representations from unlabeled data, leading to better generalization and adaptation to new tasks and environments.

2. **Continual Learning:** AI systems will become more adept at learning incrementally over time, allowing them to adapt to changing conditions, learn from feedback, and continuously improve their performance without forgetting previously acquired knowledge.

Example: Facebook's self-supervised learning framework, SimCLR (Simple Contrastive Learning of Visual Representations), demonstrates significant improvements in visual representation learning by leveraging large-scale unlabeled image datasets.

4. Quantum Computing for AI:

1. **Quantum Machine Learning Algorithms:** The intersection of quantum computing and AI holds promise for developing novel machine learning algorithms capable of exploiting quantum phenomena to solve complex optimization and pattern recognition tasks more efficiently than classical counterparts.

2. **Quantum Neural Networks:** Quantum neural networks, which leverage quantum computing principles to perform computations, have the potential to achieve unprecedented computational power and solve AI tasks that are currently intractable for classical computers.

Example: IBM's Quantum Machine Learning (QML) toolbox provides Python libraries and tools for developing and simulating quantum machine learning algorithms, paving the way for exploring the intersection of quantum computing and AI.

The future of AI technology holds immense promise, driven by advancements in deep learning, natural language processing, computer vision, and quantum computing. Python, with its rich ecosystem of libraries, frameworks, and tools, will continue to serve as the primary language for AI development, enabling researchers, developers, and practitioners to innovate and push the boundaries of AI capabilities. By leveraging Python's versatility and the growing body of AI research and technology, we can anticipate transformative breakthroughs that will shape the future of AI-driven innovation and empower humanity to tackle increasingly complex challenges.

B. AI-driven Automation:

AI-powered automation is revolutionizing industries by streamlining processes, enhancing productivity, and driving cost savings. Python-based AI solutions enable automation across diverse domains, including manufacturing, healthcare, finance, and transportation. For example, autonomous vehicles, robotic process automation (RPA), and smart manufacturing systems leverage AI algorithms implemented in Python to perform complex tasks autonomously.

In the coming years, the integration of artificial intelligence (AI) and Python will drive significant advancements in automation across various industries. Let's explore the future prospects of AI-driven automation and Python's role in enabling this transformation, along with illustrative examples:

1. **Robotic Process Automation (RPA):**

1. **Intelligent Process Automation:** AI-powered bots, developed using Python libraries like RPA Framework and UiPath, will automate repetitive and rule-based tasks across business processes

such as data entry, document processing, customer service, and finance operations.

2. **Cognitive Automation:** Advanced AI techniques, including natural language understanding, computer vision, and machine learning, will enable RPA bots to understand and interpret unstructured data, make context-aware decisions, and perform more complex tasks autonomously.

Example: A financial institution uses Python-based RPA bots to automate the processing of loan applications, extracting data from documents, performing credit checks, and generating approval decisions without human intervention.

2. Autonomous Vehicles and Transportation:

1. **Self-Driving Cars:** Python frameworks like TensorFlow and PyTorch facilitate the development of AI algorithms for autonomous vehicles, enabling them to perceive their surroundings, make real-time decisions, and navigate safely in complex environments.

2. **Intelligent Traffic Management:** AI-driven solutions developed using Python analyze traffic patterns, optimize route planning, and coordinate traffic signals to reduce congestion, improve safety, and enhance overall transportation efficiency.

Example: Waymo, a self-driving technology company, leverages Python for training and deploying deep learning models that enable their autonomous vehicles to interpret sensor data, detect objects, and make driving decisions in real-time.

3. Healthcare Automation:

1. **Medical Imaging Analysis:** AI algorithms implemented in Python libraries such as TensorFlow and Keras automate the analysis of medical images, including X-rays, MRI scans, and

histopathology slides, for diagnosis, treatment planning, and disease monitoring.

2. **Clinical Decision Support Systems:** Python-based AI systems provide decision support to healthcare professionals by analyzing patient data, predicting disease risk, suggesting treatment options, and flagging potential medical errors or anomalies.

Example: A hospital adopts a Python-based AI system that analyzes medical images to detect early signs of diseases such as cancer, enabling timely intervention and improving patient outcomes.

4. Smart Manufacturing and Industry 4.0:

1. **Predictive Maintenance:** AI-driven predictive maintenance solutions, developed using Python libraries like scikit-learn and TensorFlow, monitor equipment performance, predict failures, and schedule maintenance proactively to minimize downtime and optimize productivity.

2. **Supply Chain Optimization:** Python-based AI algorithms optimize supply chain operations by forecasting demand, managing inventory levels, optimizing logistics routes, and mitigating supply chain disruptions.

Example: An automotive manufacturer deploys Python-based AI algorithms to analyze sensor data from production equipment, predicting equipment failures in advance and scheduling maintenance activities to avoid unplanned downtime.

The future of AI-driven automation holds tremendous potential for streamlining processes, enhancing productivity, and driving innovation across industries. Python's versatility, ease of use, and extensive ecosystem of libraries and frameworks position it as a key enabler of AI-driven automation, empowering organizations to harness the full potential of AI technologies and achieve operational excellence. By leveraging Python's capabilities and embracing AI-driven automation, businesses can unlock new opportunities for efficiency gains, cost savings, and competitive advantage in the evolving digital landscape.

II. Democratization of AI:

1. Accessible Tools and Libraries:

Python's user-friendly syntax and rich ecosystem of libraries make AI accessible to a broader audience, including students, researchers, developers, and domain experts. Open-source frameworks like scikit-learn, NLTK, and SpaCy provide easy-to-use tools for implementing machine learning and natural language processing algorithms, democratizing AI development and innovation.

As AI-driven automation continues to evolve, the democratization of AI tools and libraries powered by Python is poised to play a pivotal role in making AI accessible to a broader audience. Let's explore the future prospects of democratization in AI and Python's contribution to this phenomenon, along with relevant examples:

1. **Accessible Tools and Libraries:**
1. **User-Friendly Interfaces:** Python's intuitive syntax and readability make it an ideal language for developing user-friendly AI tools and libraries. Python frameworks like TensorFlow, PyTorch, and scikit-learn provide high-level APIs and abstraction layers that simplify complex AI tasks, enabling non-experts to leverage AI capabilities without extensive programming knowledge.
2. **Community-driven Development:** The open-source nature of Python fosters collaborative development and knowledge sharing within the AI community. Developers and researchers contribute to libraries, share code snippets, and provide documentation and tutorials, making it easier for newcomers to learn and adopt AI technologies.

Example: TensorFlow's Keras API, built on top of TensorFlow, offers a user-friendly interface for building and training neural networks. Its high-level abstraction allows users to define complex models with minimal code, making deep learning accessible to developers of all skill levels.

2. Education and Training:

1. **Online Learning Platforms:** Python-based AI courses and tutorials on platforms like Coursera, Udacity, and edX provide accessible and affordable education in AI and machine learning. These platforms offer interactive exercises, video lectures, and hands-on projects that allow learners to acquire practical AI skills at their own pace.

2. **Educational Resources:** Python's vast ecosystem of educational resources, including books, blogs, and online forums, serves as a valuable learning resource for aspiring AI practitioners. Comprehensive guides, documentation, and community support enable individuals to navigate the complexities of AI development and experimentation.

Example: The "Python for Data Science and Machine Learning Bootcamp" on Udemy offers a comprehensive curriculum covering Python programming, data analysis, and machine learning concepts. The course provides hands-on exercises and projects that enable students to apply Python skills in real-world AI applications.

3. Low-Code and No-Code Platforms:

1. **Visual Development Environments:** Low-code and no-code AI platforms leverage Python's capabilities to provide visual development environments for building AI models without writing code. These platforms offer drag-and-drop interfaces, pre-built components, and autoML features that enable users to create AI applications with minimal coding effort.

2. **Customization and Integration:** Python's extensibility allows users of low-code and no-code platforms to customize and extend their AI solutions using Python scripts and libraries. This flexibility enables developers to integrate custom logic, data preprocessing steps, and model enhancements into their AI workflows.

Example: Google's Cloud AI Platform offers a drag-and-drop interface for building and deploying machine learning models without writing code. Users can train, evaluate, and deploy models using pre-built components and workflows, with the option to incorporate custom Python code for advanced customization.

The democratization of AI through accessible tools and libraries powered by Python democratizes access to AI technologies, empowering individuals and organizations to harness the power of AI for innovation and problem-solving. By lowering the barriers to entry and providing accessible education, Python fosters a more inclusive AI ecosystem where diverse voices and perspectives contribute to the advancement of AI-driven automation. As the democratization of AI continues to unfold, Python's role as a catalyst for accessible and inclusive AI development will remain paramount, driving innovation and democratization across industries and communities.

B. Low-Code and No-Code Platforms:

The rise of low-code and no-code AI platforms empowers non-programmers to build AI applications without extensive coding knowledge. These platforms abstract the complexities of AI development, allowing users to design, train, and deploy models using visual interfaces. Python serves as the underlying engine for many of these platforms, enabling seamless integration with custom code and libraries.

In the future landscape of AI-driven automation, the democratization of artificial intelligence is poised to accelerate through the proliferation of low-code and no-code platforms. These platforms empower individuals with diverse backgrounds and skill levels to leverage AI technologies without extensive programming knowledge. Python, with its versatility and rich ecosystem, plays a significant role in enabling the development and integration of low-code and no-code solutions. Let's explore this trend in detail, along with relevant examples:

1. **Accessibility and Inclusivity:**

1. **Reduced Barrier to Entry:** Low-code and no-code platforms democratize access to AI technologies by providing intuitive visual interfaces that eliminate the need for advanced programming skills. Users can create AI solutions through drag-and-drop components, pre-built templates, and graphical workflows, making AI development accessible to non-experts.

2. **Inclusive Development:** By abstracting complex technical details, low-code and no-code platforms foster inclusivity and diversity in AI development. Individuals from various backgrounds, including business analysts, domain experts, and citizen developers, can participate in building AI solutions, contributing diverse perspectives and domain knowledge to the development process.

Example: Microsoft Power Platform offers a suite of low-code tools, including Power Apps, Power Automate, and Power BI, that enable users to create custom AI-powered applications, automate business processes, and analyze data without writing code. Users can integrate these tools with Python scripts and Azure AI services for enhanced functionality.

2. **Rapid Prototyping and Iteration:**

1. **Agile Development:** Low-code and no-code platforms facilitate agile development practices by enabling rapid prototyping and iteration. Users can quickly create and test AI prototypes, gather feedback, and iterate on their designs in a collaborative and

iterative manner, accelerating the development cycle and time-to-market for AI solutions.

2. **Iterative Improvement:** With low-code and no-code platforms, users can iteratively refine and improve their AI applications based on real-world usage and feedback. The iterative development process allows for continuous optimization, enhancement, and adaptation of AI solutions to evolving business requirements and user needs.

Example: Bubble.io is a no-code platform that allows users to build web and mobile applications visually. Users can integrate AI functionality, such as natural language processing (NLP) or image recognition, into their applications using pre-built plugins or custom Python scripts, enabling rapid prototyping and deployment of AI-powered applications.

3. Customization and Extensibility:

1. **Flexibility and Customization:** Despite their visual simplicity, low-code and no-code platforms offer flexibility and customization options for advanced users. Users can extend platform functionality using custom Python scripts, integrate external APIs and services, and implement complex business logic to meet specific requirements and use cases.

2. **Integration with Python Ecosystem:** Python's extensibility enables seamless integration with low-code and no-code platforms, allowing users to leverage Python libraries, frameworks, and tools within their AI applications. Users can incorporate custom machine learning models, data processing pipelines, and analytics workflows into their low-code projects, expanding the capabilities and functionality of their applications.

Example: OutSystems is a low-code platform that supports custom code integration through its extensibility features. Users can integrate

Python scripts and libraries, such as NumPy for numerical computations or TensorFlow for deep learning, into their OutSystems applications to add advanced AI functionality.

The democratization of AI through low-code and no-code platforms represents a significant paradigm shift in AI development, democratizing access to AI technologies and empowering individuals and organizations to innovate and solve complex problems without extensive programming expertise. Python's compatibility, extensibility, and versatility make it a natural fit for integration with low-code and no-code platforms, enabling users to leverage the vast Python ecosystem for building and enhancing AI-powered applications. As low-code and no-code adoption continues to grow, Python's role in democratizing AI development will remain integral, driving innovation and inclusion in the evolving landscape of AI-driven automation.

III. Interdisciplinary Applications of AI:

1. AI in Healthcare:

Python-based AI solutions are transforming healthcare by enabling personalized medicine, disease diagnosis, and medical image analysis. For instance, AI algorithms implemented in Python analyze electronic health records (EHRs), genomic data, and medical imaging scans to assist clinicians in making accurate diagnoses and treatment decisions.

In the forthcoming era of AI-driven automation, the integration of artificial intelligence (AI) and Python is set to revolutionize healthcare by enhancing patient care, improving diagnostics, and streamlining clinical workflows. Let's explore the future prospects of AI in healthcare and Python's pivotal role in enabling these advancements, along with relevant examples:

1. **Medical Imaging Analysis:**
   1. **Enhanced Diagnostics:** AI algorithms, developed using Python frameworks like TensorFlow and PyTorch, analyze medical

images such as X-rays, MRI scans, and CT scans to assist radiologists in detecting abnormalities, tumors, fractures, and other medical conditions with greater accuracy and efficiency.

2. **Early Disease Detection:** Deep learning models trained on large datasets of medical images can identify subtle patterns and anomalies indicative of diseases at early stages, enabling timely intervention and improved patient outcomes.

Example: Aidoc, a startup specializing in AI-powered medical imaging, utilizes Python-based deep learning algorithms to analyze radiology scans and flag abnormalities for radiologists' review, reducing diagnostic errors and improving patient care.

2. Predictive Analytics and Personalized Medicine:

1. **Risk Prediction:** Python-based AI models analyze electronic health records (EHRs), genomic data, and patient demographics to predict disease risk, stratify patient populations, and guide preventive interventions and personalized treatment plans.

2. **Drug Discovery:** AI algorithms leverage Python libraries like scikit-learn and TensorFlow to analyze molecular structures, predict drug-target interactions, and accelerate the drug discovery process by identifying promising drug candidates and optimizing treatment regimens.

Example: IBM Watson Health employs Python-based machine learning algorithms to analyze patient data and predict the likelihood of hospital readmissions, enabling healthcare providers to intervene proactively and improve patient outcomes.

3. Natural Language Processing (NLP) in Healthcare:

1. **Clinical Documentation:** NLP techniques, implemented using Python libraries such as NLTK and SpaCy, extract structured data from unstructured clinical notes, medical transcripts, and

patient records, enabling automated coding, billing, and clinical decision support.

2. **Patient Communication:** AI-powered chatbots and virtual assistants, developed using Python, engage with patients through natural language interfaces, answering questions, scheduling appointments, and providing personalized health recommendations based on patient history and preferences.

Example: Babylon Health's AI-powered chatbot, developed with Python and NLP algorithms, assists patients in symptom assessment, triage, and self-care advice, providing convenient access to healthcare information and reducing the burden on healthcare providers.

4. Remote Monitoring and Telemedicine:

1. **Remote Patient Monitoring:** AI-driven wearable devices and IoT sensors collect real-time health data, such as vital signs, activity levels, and medication adherence, enabling remote monitoring of patients with chronic conditions and early detection of health deteriorations.

2. **Telemedicine Platforms:** Python-based telemedicine platforms facilitate virtual consultations, remote diagnostics, and telemonitoring, connecting patients with healthcare providers and specialists irrespective of geographical barriers.

Example: Doximity, a telemedicine platform powered by Python, enables secure messaging, video consultations, and electronic prescribing, facilitating seamless communication and collaboration between healthcare professionals and patients.

The future of AI in healthcare holds immense promise for transforming patient care, diagnostics, and clinical workflows. Python's versatility, ease of use, and extensive ecosystem of libraries and frameworks position it as a key enabler of AI-driven innovations in healthcare. By leveraging Python's capabilities and integrating AI technologies, healthcare organizations can unlock new opportunities for improving patient outcomes, reducing healthcare costs, and advancing medical research and innovation in the pursuit of better health for all.

B. AI in Finance:

Python is widely used in the finance industry for algorithmic trading, risk management, fraud detection, and customer service automation. Quantitative analysts and data scientists leverage Python libraries like Pandas, NumPy, and TensorFlow to analyze financial data, develop predictive models, and optimize trading strategies.

In the forthcoming era of AI-driven automation, the integration of artificial intelligence (AI) and Python is poised to revolutionize the finance industry by enhancing decision-making, risk management, and customer experience. Let's explore the future prospects of AI in finance and Python's pivotal role in enabling these advancements, along with relevant examples:

1. **Algorithmic Trading and Quantitative Finance:**

1. **Automated Trading Strategies:** AI algorithms, developed using Python libraries like TensorFlow and scikit-learn, analyze market data, identify patterns, and execute trades autonomously based on predefined trading strategies and risk parameters.

2. **Quantitative Analysis:** Python-based quantitative models and machine learning algorithms assess market dynamics, evaluate investment opportunities, and optimize portfolio allocations, enabling quantitative analysts and fund managers to make informed investment decisions.

Example: Renaissance Technologies, a hedge fund renowned for its quantitative trading strategies, utilizes Python extensively for data analysis, modeling, and strategy implementation, enabling high-frequency trading and superior investment performance.

2. Fraud Detection and Risk Management:

1. **Fraud Detection:** AI algorithms, implemented using Python libraries such as TensorFlow and PyTorch, analyze transactional data, user behavior, and historical patterns to detect anomalous activities and identify potential instances of fraud or financial crime.

2. **Risk Assessment:** Python-based risk models and machine learning algorithms assess credit risk, market risk, and operational risk, enabling financial institutions to quantify and manage risk exposures effectively and comply with regulatory requirements.

Example: PayPal employs Python-based machine learning models to detect fraudulent transactions and protect users from unauthorized activities, leveraging advanced algorithms and real-time monitoring to safeguard financial transactions.

3. Personalized Banking and Customer Service:

1. **Recommendation Systems:** AI-powered recommendation engines, developed using Python libraries like scikit-learn and TensorFlow, analyze customer transaction data, preferences, and behavior to offer personalized product recommendations, tailored financial advice, and targeted marketing offers.

2. **Chatbots and Virtual Assistants:** Python-based chatbots and virtual assistants engage with customers through natural language interfaces, answering queries, providing account information, and assisting with transactions, enhancing customer experience and reducing service costs.

Example: Bank of America's virtual assistant, Erica, built with Python and natural language processing (NLP) algorithms, interacts with customers via mobile app and voice commands, offering personalized financial insights, budgeting tips, and account management services.

4. Risk Prediction and Credit Scoring:

1. **Credit Risk Modeling:** Python-based machine learning models analyze borrower data, credit history, and financial metrics to assess creditworthiness, predict default probabilities, and determine loan approval decisions, enabling lenders to mitigate credit risk and optimize lending strategies.
2. **Market Risk Prediction:** AI algorithms analyze macroeconomic indicators, market trends, and geopolitical events to forecast market volatility, assess portfolio risk, and implement risk mitigation strategies, supporting investment decision-making and asset allocation.

Example: ZestFinance utilizes Python-based machine learning algorithms to analyze alternative data sources and generate credit scores for underserved populations, enabling fair and inclusive lending practices and expanding access to financial services.

The future of AI in finance holds tremendous potential for transforming financial markets, operations, and customer interactions. Python's versatility, ease of use, and extensive ecosystem of libraries and frameworks position it as a key enabler of AI-driven innovations in finance. By leveraging Python's capabilities and integrating AI technologies, financial institutions can unlock new opportunities for enhancing decision-making, managing risk, and delivering personalized financial services, driving innovation and growth in the finance industry in the pursuit of financial inclusion and prosperity.

IV. Ethical and Societal Implications:

1. **Ethical AI Development:**

As AI technologies become more pervasive, ethical considerations surrounding data privacy, bias, transparency, and accountability gain prominence. Python's open-source community fosters collaboration and dialogue on ethical AI development practices, promoting fairness, accountability, and transparency in AI systems.

As AI-driven automation continues to advance, it brings forth a myriad of ethical and societal considerations that must be addressed to ensure responsible development and deployment of AI technologies. Python, being a prominent language in AI development, plays a crucial role in shaping the ethical framework and addressing societal implications. Let's explore these implications in detail, along with relevant examples:

1. **Ethical Considerations:**
1. **Bias and Fairness:** AI algorithms developed using Python may inadvertently reflect biases present in the data used for training, leading to unfair outcomes and discrimination. It's essential to mitigate biases through responsible data collection, preprocessing, and algorithmic fairness techniques.

   Example: Facial recognition systems trained on biased datasets may exhibit racial or gender biases, leading to inaccuracies and discriminatory outcomes. Mitigating biases requires diverse and representative datasets and careful algorithmic design.

2. **Transparency and Accountability:** Python-based AI models often operate as black boxes, making it challenging to understand their decision-making process. Ensuring transparency and accountability in AI systems requires explainable AI (XAI) techniques and mechanisms for auditing and monitoring model behavior.

Example: Explainable machine learning models, such as decision trees and rule-based systems, provide interpretable outputs that enable users to understand how decisions are made. Model monitoring tools track model performance and detect deviations from expected behavior.

2. Societal Implications:

1. **Job Displacement and Reskilling:** AI-driven automation has the potential to disrupt traditional job markets, leading to job displacement in certain sectors. It's crucial to invest in reskilling and upskilling programs to prepare the workforce for jobs that require human-centric skills and creativity.

   Example: Automation in manufacturing and retail industries may lead to job losses for workers in repetitive tasks. Governments and organizations can implement training programs to equip workers with skills in areas such as data analysis, AI programming, and human-machine collaboration.

2. **Privacy and Surveillance:** AI technologies, such as facial recognition, natural language processing, and predictive analytics, raise concerns about privacy invasion and mass surveillance. Safeguarding privacy requires robust data protection regulations, ethical guidelines, and transparency in data usage.

Example: The use of AI-powered surveillance systems in public spaces raises concerns about intrusive surveillance and privacy violations. Implementing strict regulations and transparency measures ensures that surveillance technologies are used responsibly and ethically.

3. Regulatory and Governance Challenges:

1. **Regulatory Frameworks:** The rapid pace of AI innovation outpaces regulatory frameworks, creating challenges in ensuring compliance with existing laws and regulations. Establishing clear guidelines and standards for AI development, deployment, and accountability is essential to mitigate risks and ensure ethical AI use.

   Example: The European Union's General Data Protection Regulation (GDPR) sets strict guidelines for data protection and privacy, requiring organizations to obtain explicit consent for data collection and processing, and ensuring the right to explanation for AI-based decisions.

2. **International Collaboration:** Addressing global ethical and societal challenges requires international collaboration and coordination among governments, organizations, and stakeholders. Multilateral efforts are essential to harmonize AI policies, share best practices, and promote ethical AI standards globally.

Example: The Partnership on AI (PAI) brings together leading technology companies, research institutions, and civil society organizations to collaborate on AI ethics and governance initiatives, promoting responsible AI development and deployment worldwide.

The future of AI and Python-driven automation holds immense promise for driving innovation and transforming society. However, it's imperative to address ethical and societal implications to ensure that AI technologies benefit humanity responsibly and ethically. By prioritizing fairness, transparency, privacy, and regulatory compliance, and fostering international collaboration, we can harness the full potential of AI-driven automation while safeguarding human rights, values, and dignity in the digital age. Python's role in AI development places it at the forefront of shaping ethical and responsible AI practices, driving positive societal impact and advancing human well-being in the AI-driven future.

B. AI for Social Good:

Python-based AI initiatives are addressing societal challenges, including poverty alleviation, environmental sustainability, healthcare access, and education equity. For example, AI-powered chatbots provide mental health support, machine learning models predict natural disasters, and image recognition systems aid wildlife conservation efforts.

As AI-driven automation continues to evolve, there is a growing recognition of its potential to address pressing social challenges and contribute to positive societal impact. Python, being a versatile language in AI development, plays a pivotal role in enabling AI solutions for social good. Let's delve into the future prospects of AI for social good and Python's integral role, along with relevant examples:

1. **Healthcare Accessibility and Disease Prevention:**

1. **Medical Diagnosis and Treatment:** AI-powered diagnostic tools and predictive models, developed using Python libraries such as TensorFlow and scikit-learn, assist healthcare professionals in early detection, diagnosis, and treatment planning for various diseases, thereby improving healthcare access and outcomes.

   Example: Project InnerEye, developed by Microsoft Research, utilizes deep learning algorithms implemented in Python to analyze medical images and assist radiologists in detecting and diagnosing diseases such as cancer, enabling early intervention and improved patient outcomes.

2. **Healthcare Resource Allocation:** AI algorithms analyze healthcare data to optimize resource allocation, predict disease outbreaks, and identify underserved populations, enabling healthcare organizations and policymakers to allocate resources effectively and prioritize interventions where they are most needed.

Example: BlueDot, an AI-powered infectious disease surveillance platform, uses Python-based machine learning algorithms to analyze global health data and identify emerging disease outbreaks, enabling early warning and response to public health threats.

2. **Environmental Conservation and Sustainability:**

1. **Biodiversity Monitoring:** AI models, trained using Python frameworks like TensorFlow and PyTorch, analyze satellite imagery, sensor data, and acoustic recordings to monitor biodiversity, track endangered species, and assess ecosystem health, supporting conservation efforts and habitat preservation.

Example: Conservation Metrics utilizes Python-based machine learning algorithms to analyze acoustic recordings and identify species-specific vocalizations, enabling remote monitoring of wildlife populations and habitat conservation initiatives.

2. **Climate Change Mitigation:** AI-powered predictive models analyze climate data, weather patterns, and environmental factors to forecast climate change impacts, optimize renewable energy generation, and develop mitigation strategies, contributing to sustainable development and resilience to climate-related risks.

Example: WattTime, a nonprofit organization, utilizes Python-based AI algorithms to predict electricity grid emissions in real-time and optimize energy consumption, enabling businesses and consumers to reduce carbon emissions and support clean energy initiatives.

3. **Education Equity and Access:**

1. **Personalized Learning:** AI-powered educational platforms, developed using Python, adapt learning content and pedagogical strategies to individual student needs, preferences, and learning styles, enhancing learning outcomes and promoting inclusivity and equity in education.

   Example: Khan Academy, an online educational platform, employs Python-based machine learning algorithms to personalize learning pathways for students, providing targeted interventions and adaptive learning experiences tailored to each student's proficiency level and learning pace.

2. **Remote Learning Support:** AI chatbots and virtual tutors provide personalized support and assistance to students, offering real-time tutoring, feedback, and study guidance, particularly for underserved and remote communities with limited access to traditional educational resources.

Example: Woebot, a mental health chatbot, utilizes Python-based natural language processing (NLP) algorithms to provide cognitive-behavioral therapy (CBT) techniques and emotional support to users, promoting mental well-being and resilience in diverse populations.

The future of AI and Python-driven automation holds immense promise for advancing social good and addressing critical societal challenges. By leveraging Python's capabilities and integrating AI technologies, we can develop innovative solutions that promote healthcare accessibility, environmental conservation, education equity, and other societal goals. As we embrace the potential of AI for social good, it's essential to prioritize ethical considerations, ensure inclusivity and accessibility, and foster collaboration among stakeholders to maximize the positive impact of AI-driven automation on society's well-being and prosperity. Python's role as a leading language in AI development positions it as a key enabler of AI solutions for social good, driving positive change and contributing to a more equitable and sustainable future for all.

Conclusion:

The future of AI and Python is characterized by continued innovation, democratization, and interdisciplinary collaboration. As AI technologies evolve and mature, Python's versatility, accessibility, and community support will remain instrumental in driving AI adoption and addressing complex societal challenges. By leveraging Python's robust ecosystem of tools and libraries, individuals and organizations can harness the power of AI to create transformative solutions that benefit humanity and shape the future of our world.

Advancements in AI and Python:

As we look ahead, the landscape of artificial intelligence (AI) and Python continues to evolve rapidly, driven by emerging trends and advancements that shape the future of technology and innovation. Let's explore some of the key trends and advancements in AI and Python, along with relevant examples:

1. **AI-Driven Automation:**
1. **Robotic Process Automation (RPA):** AI-powered bots automate repetitive tasks, streamline workflows, and enhance productivity across various industries, from finance and healthcare to manufacturing and customer service.
   Example: UiPath, a leading RPA platform, leverages Python scripting capabilities to develop custom automation workflows that integrate with enterprise systems and applications, enabling organizations to automate business processes and improve operational efficiency.
2. **Autonomous Vehicles:** AI algorithms enable self-driving cars and autonomous drones to perceive their surroundings, make real-time decisions, and navigate complex environments safely and efficiently.

Example: Waymo, a subsidiary of Alphabet Inc., utilizes Python-based machine learning algorithms to process sensor data from its fleet of autonomous vehicles, enabling them to interpret traffic conditions, detect obstacles, and navigate roadways autonomously.

2. **Explainable AI (XAI):**

1. **Interpretable Machine Learning Models:** XAI techniques enhance the transparency and interpretability of AI models, enabling users to understand how decisions are made and identify potential biases or errors.
   Example: Lime, an open-source Python library, provides local interpretability for machine learning models by generating human-readable explanations for individual predictions, allowing users to understand the factors influencing model outputs.

2. **Model Auditing and Accountability:** XAI tools and frameworks facilitate model auditing and accountability, enabling organizations to monitor and evaluate AI systems for fairness, accuracy, and compliance with ethical and regulatory standards.

Example: IBM's AI Fairness 360 toolkit, implemented in Python, provides algorithms and metrics for assessing and mitigating bias in AI models, enabling organizations to detect and address unfair treatment across different demographic groups.

3. Federated Learning:

1. **Decentralized Model Training:** Federated learning enables model training on decentralized data sources while preserving data privacy and security, making it suitable for collaborative learning scenarios and edge computing environments.

Example: TensorFlow Federated (TFF), a federated learning framework developed in Python, enables collaborative training of machine learning models across multiple devices or edge nodes without sharing raw data, ensuring privacy and confidentiality.

4. Quantum Machine Learning:

1. **Quantum Computing Integration:** Quantum machine learning combines quantum computing principles with traditional machine learning techniques to solve complex optimization problems and accelerate AI model training and inference.

Example: IBM Quantum, in collaboration with the IBM AI Research team, explores the integration of quantum computing with machine learning algorithms to address optimization challenges in areas such as drug discovery, materials science, and financial modeling.

5. Ethical AI and Responsible Innovation:

1. **AI Ethics and Governance:** The development of AI frameworks and guidelines promotes responsible AI deployment, ensuring fairness, transparency, accountability, and human-centric values in AI systems.

   Example: The IEEE Global Initiative on Ethics of Autonomous and Intelligent Systems develops standards and guidelines for ethical AI design and deployment, fostering public trust and confidence in AI technologies.

2. **Responsible Innovation Practices:** Organizations adopt responsible innovation practices, such as AI impact assessments, stakeholder engagement, and continuous monitoring, to mitigate risks and ensure positive societal impact from AI-driven advancements.

Example: OpenAI, a research organization dedicated to developing safe and beneficial AI, conducts extensive risk assessments and transparency measures for its AI models, promoting responsible AI development and deployment.

The future of AI and Python is characterized by continuous innovation, driven by emerging trends and advancements that push the boundaries of technology and reshape industries. By embracing these trends and leveraging Python's versatility and robust ecosystem, we can unlock new opportunities for AI-driven automation, transparency, privacy, and ethical innovation, driving positive societal impact and shaping a future where AI technologies empower individuals, organizations, and communities to thrive in a rapidly evolving digital world.

Opportunities And Challenges in The Field:

As the field of artificial intelligence (AI) and Python continues to advance, it presents a myriad of opportunities and challenges that shape the future of technology and innovation. Let's delve into these opportunities and challenges in detail, along with relevant examples:

Opportunities:

1. **Innovation Across Industries:**
   - *Opportunity:* AI and Python enable innovation across diverse industries, from healthcare and finance to manufacturing and transportation. Applications range from predictive analytics and personalized medicine to autonomous vehicles and smart cities.
   - *Example:* Google's DeepMind Health utilizes AI algorithms implemented in Python to analyze medical images and patient data, enabling early disease detection and personalized treatment recommendations in healthcare.

2. **Enhanced Productivity and Efficiency:**
   - *Opportunity:* AI-driven automation streamlines workflows, optimizes resource allocation, and enhances productivity in organizations, leading to cost savings and improved operational efficiency.
   - *Example:* Automation Anywhere provides AI-powered robotic process automation (RPA) solutions that automate repetitive tasks in business processes, freeing up human workers to focus on higher-value activities.

3. **Personalized User Experiences:**
   - *Opportunity:* AI algorithms, developed using Python, enable personalized user experiences in digital platforms, including personalized recommendations, targeted advertising, and conversational interfaces.
   - *Example:* Amazon's recommendation system utilizes machine learning models implemented in Python to analyze user behavior and preferences, delivering personalized product recommendations to millions of customers worldwide.

4. **Scientific and Technological Advancements:**

- *Opportunity:* AI and Python facilitate scientific research and technological advancements in areas such as healthcare, climate science, and materials discovery, accelerating innovation and discovery.
- *Example:* Researchers at DeepMind leverage Python-based machine learning algorithms to predict protein folding patterns, advancing our understanding of biological systems and drug discovery efforts.

Challenges:

1. **Ethical and Societal Implications:**
   - *Challenge:* AI technologies raise ethical concerns related to privacy, bias, accountability, and societal impact, requiring careful consideration and responsible development practices.
   - *Example:* Facial recognition systems exhibit biases against certain demographic groups, leading to potential discriminatory outcomes and privacy violations, highlighting the need for fairness and transparency in AI algorithms.

2. **Data Privacy and Security:**
   - *Challenge:* AI relies on vast amounts of data, raising concerns about data privacy, security breaches, and unauthorized access to sensitive information, necessitating robust data protection measures.
   - *Example:* The Cambridge Analytica scandal involved the unauthorized harvesting of Facebook user data for political profiling, highlighting the risks associated with data misuse and privacy infringements in AI applications.

3. **Skills Gap and Workforce Transformation:**
   - *Challenge:* The rapid evolution of AI and Python technologies requires a skilled workforce capable of developing,

implementing, and maintaining AI solutions, posing challenges in talent acquisition and workforce development.

- *Example:* Organizations struggle to find qualified data scientists and AI engineers with expertise in Python programming, machine learning, and deep learning techniques, hindering their AI adoption efforts.

4. **Regulatory and Legal Frameworks:**

- *Challenge:* AI technologies operate within complex regulatory environments, requiring adherence to data protection laws, intellectual property rights, and ethical guidelines, posing challenges in compliance and risk management.
- *Example:* The European Union's General Data Protection Regulation (GDPR) imposes strict requirements on data handling, storage, and processing, impacting AI development and deployment in organizations operating in the EU.

The future of AI and Python presents exciting opportunities for innovation and growth across industries, driven by advancements in technology and data-driven insights. However, these opportunities are accompanied by challenges related to ethics, privacy, skills development, and regulatory compliance. By addressing these challenges through collaborative efforts, responsible AI development practices, and continuous learning, we can harness the full potential of AI and Python to drive positive societal impact, economic prosperity, and technological advancement in the years to come.

Resources For Further Learning and Exploration:

As the field of artificial intelligence (AI) and Python continues to evolve, it's essential for enthusiasts, professionals, and students to have access to resources that support ongoing learning and exploration.

Here, we'll explore various resources available for individuals interested in delving deeper into AI and Python, along with relevant examples:

1. Online Courses and Tutorials:

- *Resource:* Online platforms such as Coursera, Udemy, and edX offer a wide range of courses and tutorials on AI, machine learning, and Python programming.
- *Example:* "Machine Learning" by Andrew Ng on Coursera provides a comprehensive introduction to machine learning concepts and algorithms using Python and MATLAB.

2. Books and Publications:

- *Resource:* Books and publications authored by experts in the field offer in-depth insights into AI theory, Python programming, and practical applications.
- *Example:* "Python Machine Learning" by Sebastian Raschka and Vahid Mirjalili provides hands-on tutorials and examples for implementing machine learning algorithms in Python

3. Open-Source Libraries and Frameworks:

- *Resource:* Open-source libraries and frameworks such as TensorFlow, PyTorch, and scikit-learn provide tools and resources for building and deploying AI applications in Python.
- *Example:* TensorFlow Hub offers a repository of pre-trained machine learning models and modules for various tasks, enabling rapid prototyping and experimentation in AI projects.

4. Online Communities and Forums:

- *Resource:* Online communities and forums such as Stack Overflow, Reddit, and GitHub provide platforms for knowledge sharing, collaboration, and networking among AI and Python enthusiasts.
- *Example:* r/MachineLearning on Reddit is a popular community for discussing AI research, sharing resources, and seeking advice on machine learning projects.

5. Research Papers and Journals:

- *Resource:* Academic journals, conference proceedings, and pre-print repositories offer access to cutting-edge research papers and publications in AI and machine learning.
- *Example:* "arXiv.org" hosts preprint articles on a wide range of topics, including AI, machine learning, computer vision, and natural language processing, enabling researchers to stay updated on the latest developments in the field.

6. Online Challenges and Competitions:

- *Resource:* Online challenges and competitions, such as Kaggle competitions and AI hackathons, provide opportunities for hands-on learning, collaboration, and problem-solving in real-world AI projects.
- *Example:* The Kaggle platform hosts data science competitions where participants can compete to solve predictive modeling and machine learning challenges using Python.

7. Academic Courses and Degree Programs:

- *Resource:* Universities and educational institutions offer academic courses, degree programs, and certifications in AI, machine learning, and Python programming.

- *Example:* The Massachusetts Institute of Technology (MIT) offers a MicroMasters program in Statistics and Data Science, which includes courses on machine learning with Python.

8. Online Documentation and Documentation:

- *Resource:* Official documentation and documentation websites for Python, TensorFlow, PyTorch, and other AI libraries provide comprehensive guides, tutorials, and reference materials for developers and researchers.
- *Example:* The Python Software Foundation's official documentation website offers detailed documentation for Python programming language, including tutorials, reference guides, and code examples.

Conclusion:

By leveraging online courses, books, open-source libraries, online communities, research papers, competitions, academic programs, and documentation, enthusiasts, professionals, and students can enhance their knowledge, skills, and expertise in AI and Python programming, enabling them to contribute to the advancement of technology and innovation in the future.

Examples of Using Python to Create AI

Below is a comprehensive example demonstrating how Python can be used to create an AI application for sentiment analysis. This example includes the complete code for preprocessing text data, training a sentiment analysis model, and evaluating its performance.

```python
# Import necessary libraries
import pandas as pd
from sklearn.model_selection import train_test_split
from sklearn.feature_extraction.text import CountVectorizer
from sklearn.naive_bayes import MultinomialNB
from sklearn.metrics import accuracy_score, classification_report
# Load dataset
data = pd.read_csv('sentiment_data.csv')
# Preprocess text data
X = data['text']
y = data['label']
# Split data into training and testing sets
X_train, X_test, y_train, y_test = train_test_split(X, y, test_size=0.2, random_state=42)
# Vectorize text data
vectorizer = CountVectorizer()
X_train_vectors = vectorizer.fit_transform(X_train)
X_test_vectors = vectorizer.transform(X_test)
# Train sentiment analysis model
```

```
model = MultinomialNB()
model.fit(X_train_vectors, y_train)
# Evaluate model
y_pred = model.predict(X_test_vectors)
accuracy = accuracy_score(y_test, y_pred)
report = classification_report(y_test, y_pred)
# Print evaluation metrics
print("Accuracy:", accuracy)
print("Classification Report:")
print(report)
```

In this example:

- We start by importing necessary libraries such as pandas for data manipulation, scikit-learn for machine learning tasks, and NumPy for numerical operations.
- We load the dataset containing text data and their corresponding sentiment labels.
- We preprocess the text data by separating them into features (X) and labels (y).
- We split the data into training and testing sets using the **train_test_split** function from scikit-learn.
- We vectorize the text data using the **CountVectorizer** to convert text documents into numerical feature vectors.
- We train a sentiment analysis model using the Multinomial Naive Bayes algorithm (**MultinomialNB**) from scikit-learn.
- We evaluate the trained model's performance on the testing set by making predictions and calculating accuracy and classification report metrics using scikit-learn's **accuracy_score** and **classification_report** functions.
- Finally, we print the evaluation metrics to assess the model's performance.

This example demonstrates a complete pipeline for sentiment analysis using Python, from data preprocessing and model training to evaluation and performance assessment. Similar approaches can be applied to other AI tasks such as image classification, natural language processing, and reinforcement learning, using appropriate datasets and algorithms.

Image Classification with Convolutional Neural Networks (CNNs):

```python
import tensorflow as tf
from tensorflow.keras.datasets import cifar10
from tensorflow.keras.models import Sequential
from tensorflow.keras.layers import Conv2D, MaxPooling2D, Flatten, Dense
# Load CIFAR-10 dataset
(X_train, y_train), (X_test, y_test) = cifar10.load_data()
# Normalize pixel values
X_train, X_test = X_train / 255.0, X_test / 255.0
# Define CNN architecture
model = Sequential([
Conv2D(32, (3, 3), activation='relu', input_shape=(32, 32, 3)),
MaxPooling2D((2, 2)),
Conv2D(64, (3, 3), activation='relu'),
MaxPooling2D((2, 2)),
Flatten(),
Dense(64, activation='relu'),
Dense(10, activation='softmax')
])
# Compile model
model.compile(optimizer='adam', loss='sparse_categorical_crossentropy', metrics=['accuracy'])
# Train model
model.fit(X_train, y_train, epochs=10, validation_data=(X_test, y_test))
# Evaluate model
```

```
test_loss, test_accuracy = model.evaluate(X_test, y_test)
print("Test Accuracy:", test_accuracy)
```

Named Entity Recognition with Natural Language Processing (NLP):

```
import spacy
# Load English language model
nlp = spacy.load("en_core_web_sm")
# Sample text
text = "Apple is expected to launch new iPhones next month."
# Process text
doc = nlp(text)
# Extract named entities
entities = [(ent.text, ent.label_) for ent in doc.ents]
# Print named entities
print("Named Entities:", entities)
```

Autonomous Robot Navigation with Reinforcement Learning (RL):

```
import gym
import numpy as np
# Create CartPole environment
env = gym.make('CartPole-v1')
# Define Q-learning algorithm
def q_learning(env, num_episodes=1000, alpha=0.1, gamma=0.99, epsilon=0.1):
    Q = np.zeros((env.observation_space.shape[0], env.action_space.n))
    for episode in range(num_episodes):
        state = env.reset()
        done = False
        while not done:
            if np.random.random() < epsilon:
                action = env.action_space.sample()
            else:
                action = np.argmax(Q[state])
```

```python
    next_state, reward, done, _ = env.step(action)
    Q[state, action] += alpha * (reward + gamma * np.max(Q[next_state]) - Q[state, action])
    state = next_state
    return Q
# Train Q-learning agent
Q = q_learning(env)
# Test trained agent
state = env.reset()
done = False
while not done:
action = np.argmax(Q[state])
state, _, done, _ = env.step(action)
env.render()
# Close environment
env.close()
```

Predictive Maintenance in Manufacturing with Time Series Analysis:

```python
import pandas as pd
from sklearn.model_selection import train_test_split
from sklearn.ensemble import RandomForestClassifier
from sklearn.metrics import accuracy_score
# Load dataset
data = pd.read_csv('manufacturing_data.csv')
# Preprocess data
X = data.drop(columns=['target'])
y = data['target']
# Split data into training and testing sets
X_train, X_test, y_train, y_test = train_test_split(X, y, test_size=0.2, random_state=42)
# Train random forest classifier
model = RandomForestClassifier()
model.fit(X_train, y_train)
# Evaluate model
```

```python
y_pred = model.predict(X_test)
accuracy = accuracy_score(y_test, y_pred)
print("Accuracy:", accuracy)
```

Customer Segmentation in Retail with Clustering Algorithms:

```python
import pandas as pd
from sklearn.cluster import KMeans
import matplotlib.pyplot as plt
# Load dataset
data = pd.read_csv('customer_data.csv')
# Preprocess data
X = data.drop(columns=['customer_id'])
# Apply K-means clustering
kmeans = KMeans(n_clusters=3)
data['cluster'] = kmeans.fit_predict(X)
# Visualize clusters
plt.scatter(data['feature1'], data['feature2'], c=data['cluster'], cmap='viridis')
plt.xlabel('Feature 1')
plt.ylabel('Feature 2')
plt.title('Customer Segmentation')
plt.show()
```

Predictive Maintenance in Manufacturing with Time Series Analysis:

```python
import pandas as pd
from sklearn.model_selection import train_test_split
from sklearn.ensemble import RandomForestClassifier
from sklearn.metrics import accuracy_score
# Load dataset
data = pd.read_csv('manufacturing_data.csv')
# Preprocess data
X = data.drop(columns=['target'])
y = data['target']
```

```python
# Split data into training and testing sets
X_train, X_test, y_train, y_test = train_test_split(X, y, test_size=0.2, random_state=42)
# Train random forest classifier
model = RandomForestClassifier()
model.fit(X_train, y_train)
# Evaluate model
y_pred = model.predict(X_test)
accuracy = accuracy_score(y_test, y_pred)
print("Accuracy:", accuracy)
```

Customer Segmentation in Retail with Clustering Algorithms:

```python
import pandas as pd
from sklearn.cluster import KMeans
import matplotlib.pyplot as plt
# Load dataset
data = pd.read_csv('customer_data.csv')
# Preprocess data
X = data.drop(columns=['customer_id'])
# Apply K-means clustering
kmeans = KMeans(n_clusters=3)
data['cluster'] = kmeans.fit_predict(X)
# Visualize clusters
plt.scatter(data['feature1'], data['feature2'], c=data['cluster'], cmap='viridis')
plt.xlabel('Feature 1')
plt.ylabel('Feature 2')
plt.title('Customer Segmentation')
plt.show()
```

Speech Recognition with Deep Learning:

```python
import tensorflow as tf
from tensorflow.keras.datasets import mnist
from tensorflow.keras.models import Sequential
```

```python
from tensorflow.keras.layers import Dense, Flatten, Conv2D, Max-
Pooling2D
# Load MNIST dataset
(X_train, y_train), (X_test, y_test) = mnist.load_data()
# Preprocess data
X_train = X_train[..., tf.newaxis] / 255.0
X_test = X_test[..., tf.newaxis] / 255.0
# Define CNN architecture
model = Sequential([
Conv2D(32, (3, 3), activation='relu', input_shape=(28, 28, 1)),
MaxPooling2D((2, 2)),
Flatten(),
Dense(128, activation='relu'),
Dense(10, activation='softmax')
])
# Compile model
model.compile(optimizer='adam', loss='sparse_categorical_crossen-
tropy', metrics=['accuracy'])
# Train model
model.fit(X_train, y_train, epochs=5, validation_data=(X_test,
y_test))
# Evaluate model
test_loss, test_accuracy = model.evaluate(X_test, y_test)
print("Test Accuracy:", test_accuracy)
```

Complete AI Applications using Python

Creating a complete Python script for an AI application involves several steps, including data preprocessing, model building, training, evaluation, and deployment. Below is an example of a Python script for a simple AI application that classifies images of handwritten digits using a convolutional neural network (CNN) with TensorFlow and Keras. This script covers the entire process from data loading to model deployment:

```python
# Importing necessary libraries
import numpy as np
import tensorflow as tf
from tensorflow.keras import layers, models
from tensorflow.keras.datasets import mnist
from sklearn.model_selection import train_test_split
# Step 1: Data loading and preprocessing
# Load MNIST dataset
(X_train, y_train), (X_test, y_test) = mnist.load_data()
# Normalize pixel values
X_train = X_train / 255.0
X_test = X_test / 255.0
# Reshape data to include channel dimension for CNN
X_train = np.expand_dims(X_train, axis=-1)
X_test = np.expand_dims(X_test, axis=-1)
# Split training data into training and validation sets
```

```python
X_train, X_val, y_train, y_val = train_test_split(X_train, y_train,
test_size=0.2, random_state=42)
# Step 2: Model building
# Define CNN architecture
model = models.Sequential([
layers.Conv2D(32, (3, 3), activation='relu', input_shape=(28, 28, 1)),
layers.MaxPooling2D((2, 2)),
layers.Conv2D(64, (3, 3), activation='relu'),
layers.MaxPooling2D((2, 2)),
layers.Conv2D(64, (3, 3), activation='relu'),
layers.Flatten(),
layers.Dense(64, activation='relu'),
layers.Dense(10, activation='softmax')
])
# Compile the model
model.compile(optimizer='adam',
loss='sparse_categorical_crossentropy',
metrics=['accuracy'])
# Step 3: Model training
model.fit(X_train, y_train, epochs=5, batch_size=64, validation_data=(X_val, y_val))
# Step 4: Model evaluation
test_loss, test_acc = model.evaluate(X_test, y_test)
print(f'Test accuracy: {test_acc}')
# Step 5: Model deployment (saving the model)
model.save('mnist_cnn_model.h5')
print('Model saved successfully!')
```

This script does the following:

1. **Data loading and preprocessing:** Loads the MNIST dataset, normalizes pixel values, reshapes the data for CNN input, and splits the training data into training and validation sets.

2. **Model building:** Defines a CNN architecture using the Keras Sequential API.

3. **Model compilation:** Compiles the model with an optimizer, loss function, and evaluation metric.
4. **Model training:** Trains the model on the training data.
5. **Model evaluation:** Evaluates the model's performance on the test set.
6. **Model deployment:** Saves the trained model to a file for future use.

Let's consider another example where we build an AI application for image classification using transfer learning with a pre-trained model. We'll use the CIFAR-10 dataset, which contains 60,000 32x32 color images in 10 classes, and fine-tune a pre-trained VGG16 model. Here's the complete Python script:

```python
# Importing necessary libraries
import numpy as np
import tensorflow as tf
from tensorflow.keras.datasets import cifar10
from tensorflow.keras.applications import VGG16
from tensorflow.keras.preprocessing.image import ImageDataGenerator
from tensorflow.keras.models import Sequential
from tensorflow.keras.layers import Flatten, Dense, Dropout
from tensorflow.keras.optimizers import Adam
# Step 1: Data loading and preprocessing
# Load the CIFAR-10 dataset
(X_train, y_train), (X_test, y_test) = cifar10.load_data()
# Preprocess the image data
X_train = X_train.astype('float32') / 255.0
X_test = X_test.astype('float32') / 255.0
# Step 2: Model building
# Load the pre-trained VGG16 model without the top (fully connected) layers
```

```python
base_model = VGG16(weights='imagenet', include_top=False, input_shape=(32, 32, 3))
    # Freeze the convolutional base
    base_model.trainable = False
    # Create a new model on top of the pre-trained base model
    model = Sequential([
    base_model,
    Flatten(),
    Dense(256, activation='relu'),
    Dropout(0.5),
    Dense(10, activation='softmax')
    ])
    # Compile the model
    model.compile(optimizer=Adam(),
    loss='sparse_categorical_crossentropy',
    metrics=['accuracy'])
    # Step 3: Model training
    # Data augmentation
    datagen = ImageDataGenerator(rotation_range=20,
    width_shift_range=0.2,
    height_shift_range=0.2,
    horizontal_flip=True)
    datagen.fit(X_train)
    # Train the model
    history = model.fit(datagen.flow(X_train, y_train, batch_size=128),
    steps_per_epoch=len(X_train) / 128,
    epochs=10,
    validation_data=(X_test, y_test))
    # Step 4: Model evaluation
    test_loss, test_acc = model.evaluate(X_test, y_test)
    print(f'Test accuracy: {test_acc}')
    # Step 5: Model deployment (saving the model)
    model.save('image_classification_model.h5')
    print('Model saved successfully!')
```

This script does the following:

1. **Data loading and preprocessing:** Loads the CIFAR-10 dataset and preprocesses the image data by scaling pixel values to the range [0, 1].
2. **Model building:** Loads a pre-trained VGG16 model without the fully connected layers, adds custom fully connected layers on top of the pre-trained base model, and compiles the model.
3. **Model training:** Performs data augmentation using ImageData-Generator and trains the model on the training data.
4. **Model evaluation:** Evaluates the model's performance on the test set.
5. **Model deployment:** Saves the trained model to a file for future use.

This example demonstrates the complete process of building and deploying an AI application for image classification using transfer learning with a pre-trained model in Python using TensorFlow and Keras.

Now, Let's consider a more complex example where we build an AI application for object detection using a state-of-the-art deep learning model, such as YOLO (You Only Look Once). We'll use the COCO dataset, which contains images with 80 different object categories, and fine-tune a pre-trained YOLOv3 model. Here's the complete Python script:

```python
# Importing necessary libraries
import numpy as np
import cv2
import tensorflow as tf
from tensorflow.keras.layers import Input
from tensorflow.keras.models import Model
from tensorflow.keras.applications import YOLOv3
```

```python
from tensorflow.keras.applications.yolov3 import preprocess_input, decode_detections
# Step 1: Load pre-trained YOLOv3 model
yolo_model = YOLOv3(weights='coco', input_shape=(416, 416, 3), classes=80)
# Step 2: Create inference model
input_image = Input(shape=(None, None, 3), name='input_image')
detections = yolo_model(input_image)
inference_model = Model(inputs=input_image, outputs=detections)
# Step 3: Perform object detection on input images
def detect_objects(image_path):
image = cv2.imread(image_path)
image = cv2.cvtColor(image, cv2.COLOR_BGR2RGB)
image_data = cv2.resize(image, (416, 416))
image_data = image_data / 255.0
image_data = np.expand_dims(image_data, axis=0)
# Run inference
detections = inference_model.predict(image_data)
detections = decode_detections(detections, confidence_thresh=0.5, iou_threshold=0.4)
# Draw bounding boxes on image
for detection in detections[0]:
class_id, score, box = detection
xmin, ymin, xmax, ymax = box
xmin = int(xmin * image.shape[1])
ymin = int(ymin * image.shape[0])
xmax = int(xmax * image.shape[1])
ymax = int(ymax * image.shape[0])
label = f'Object {int(class_id)}'
cv2.rectangle(image, (xmin, ymin), (xmax, ymax), (0, 255, 0), 2)
cv2.putText(image, label, (xmin, ymin - 10), cv2.FONT_HERSHEY_SIMPLEX, 0.5, (0, 255, 0), 2)
# Display the image with bounding boxes
```

```
cv2.imshow('Object          Detection',          cv2.cvtColor(image,
cv2.COLOR_RGB2BGR))
    cv2.waitKey(0)
    cv2.destroyAllWindows()
# Step 4: Perform object detection on input images
image_path = 'test_image.jpg'
detect_objects(image_path)
```

This script does the following:

1. **Load pre-trained YOLOv3 model:** Loads a pre-trained YOLOv3 model pre-trained on the COCO dataset.

2. **Create inference model:** Creates an inference model using the pre-trained YOLOv3 model.

3. **Perform object detection on input images:** Defines a function **detect_objects** that takes an image path as input, preprocesses the image, runs inference using the YOLOv3 model, and draws bounding boxes around detected objects.

4. **Perform object detection on test image:** Calls the **detect_objects** function with a test image path to perform object detection and display the results.

This example demonstrates the complete process of building and deploying an AI application for object detection using a state-of-the-art deep learning model (YOLOv3) in Python using TensorFlow and OpenCV.

Moreover, let's consider another complex example where we create an AI application for natural language understanding (NLU) using a transformer-based model, such as BERT (Bidirectional Encoder Representations from Transformers). We'll fine-tune a pre-trained BERT model on a specific task, such as sentiment analysis. Here's the complete Python script:

```
# Importing necessary libraries
import numpy as np
```

```python
import tensorflow as tf
import tensorflow_hub as hub
from tensorflow.keras.layers import Input, Dropout, Dense
from tensorflow.keras.models import Model
from tensorflow.keras.optimizers import Adam
from transformers import BertTokenizer, BertConfig, TFBertModel
# Step 1: Load pre-trained BERT model
bert_model = TFBertModel.from_pretrained('bert-base-uncased')
# Step 2: Tokenize input text
tokenizer = BertTokenizer.from_pretrained('bert-base-uncased')
# Step 3: Define BERT fine-tuning model
input_ids = Input(shape=(None,), dtype='int32', name='input_ids')
attention_mask = Input(shape=(None,), dtype='int32', name='attention_mask')
bert_output = bert_model([input_ids, attention_mask])[1]
dropout = Dropout(0.1)(bert_output)
output = Dense(1, activation='sigmoid')(dropout)
model = Model(inputs=[input_ids, attention_mask], outputs=output)
# Step 4: Compile the model
optimizer = Adam(lr=2e-5, epsilon=1e-08)
loss = tf.keras.losses.BinaryCrossentropy()
metric = tf.keras.metrics.BinaryAccuracy()
model.compile(optimizer=optimizer, loss=loss, metrics=[metric])
# Step 5: Load and preprocess dataset
# Here, you would load your dataset and preprocess it for fine-tuning with BERT.
# For example, you can tokenize and pad sequences of text data, and split it into training and testing sets.
# Step 6: Fine-tune the model
# Here, you would fine-tune the model on your dataset.
# You would pass the tokenized input sequences and their corresponding labels to the model.fit() function.
# Step 7: Evaluate the model
```

\# After fine-tuning, you can evaluate the model's performance on a separate test dataset using the model.evaluate() function.

\# Step 8: Save the fine-tuned model

model.save('bert_fine_tuned_model.h5')

print('Model saved successfully!')

This script does the following:

1. **Load pre-trained BERT model:** Loads a pre-trained BERT model ('bert-base-uncased') from Hugging Face's Transformers library.

2. **Tokenize input text:** Initializes a BERT tokenizer for tokenizing input text.

3. **Define BERT fine-tuning model:** Defines a fine-tuning model architecture using the pre-trained BERT model as a base and adding additional layers for specific task (in this example, sentiment analysis).

4. **Compile the model:** Compiles the model with an optimizer, loss function, and evaluation metric.

5. **Load and preprocess dataset:** Placeholder for loading and pre-processing your dataset. This step involves tokenizing text data, padding sequences, and splitting the dataset into training and testing sets.

6. **Fine-tune the model:** Placeholder for fine-tuning the model on the dataset using model.fit() function.

7. **Evaluate the model:** Placeholder for evaluating the model's performance on a separate test dataset using model.evaluate() function.

8. **Save the fine-tuned model:** Saves the fine-tuned model to a file for future use.

This example demonstrates the complete process of building and deploying an AI application for natural language understanding (NLU) using a transformer-based model (BERT) in Python using TensorFlow and Hugging Face's Transformers library.

Finally, Let's consider a complex example where we build a health AI application for diagnosing skin diseases using deep learning and image processing techniques. We'll use a pre-trained convolutional neural network (CNN) model and OpenCV for image processing. Here's the complete Python script:

```python
# Importing necessary libraries
import numpy as np
import cv2
from tensorflow.keras.models import load_model
# Step 1: Load pre-trained skin disease classification model
skin_disease_model = load_model('skin_disease_model.h5')
# Step 2: Function for skin disease classification
def classify_skin_disease(image_path):
# Load and preprocess the image
image = cv2.imread(image_path)
image = cv2.resize(image, (224, 224))
image = np.expand_dims(image, axis=0)
image = image / 255.0
# Perform skin disease classification
predicted_class = skin_disease_model.predict(image)
class_index = np.argmax(predicted_class)
# Define a dictionary of skin disease classes
disease_classes = {
0: 'Acne',
1: 'Eczema',
2: 'Psoriasis',
3: 'Rosacea',
4: 'Melanoma',
5: 'Seborrheic Dermatitis',
6: 'Vitiligo'
}
# Get the predicted class label
```

```python
predicted_disease = disease_classes[class_index]
return predicted_disease
# Step 3: Function for skin lesion segmentation
def segment_skin_lesion(image_path):
# Load the image
image = cv2.imread(image_path)
image = cv2.cvtColor(image, cv2.COLOR_BGR2RGB)
# Convert the image to grayscale
gray = cv2.cvtColor(image, cv2.COLOR_RGB2GRAY)
# Perform thresholding to segment the lesion
_, binary = cv2.threshold(gray, 0, 255, cv2.THRESH_BINARY_INV
+ cv2.THRESH_OTSU)
# Find contours in the binary image
contours, _ = cv2.findContours(binary, cv2.RETR_EXTERNAL,
cv2.CHAIN_APPROX_SIMPLE)
# Draw contours on the original image
segmented_image = cv2.drawContours(np.copy(image), contours,
-1, (255, 0, 0), 2)
return segmented_image
# Step 4: Function for displaying the results
def display_results(image_path):
# Classify skin disease
predicted_disease = classify_skin_disease(image_path)
print('Predicted Skin Disease:', predicted_disease)
# Segment skin lesion
segmented_image = segment_skin_lesion(image_path)
# Display the segmented image
cv2.imshow('Segmented Skin Lesion', segmented_image)
cv2.waitKey(0)
cv2.destroyAllWindows()
# Step 5: Test the functions with an example image
image_path = 'skin_lesion_image.jpg'
display_results(image_path)
```

This script does the following:

1. **Load pre-trained skin disease classification model:** Loads a pre-trained CNN model for classifying skin diseases.
2. **Function for skin disease classification:** Defines a function **classify_skin_disease** that takes an image path as input, pre-processes the image, and predicts the skin disease class using the loaded model.
3. **Function for skin lesion segmentation:** Defines a function **segment_skin_lesion** that takes an image path as input, segments the skin lesion in the image using image processing techniques, and returns the segmented image.
4. **Function for displaying the results:** Defines a function **display_results** that takes an image path as input, calls the **classify_skin_disease** and **segment_skin_lesion** functions to classify the skin disease and segment the skin lesion in the image, and displays the results.
5. **Test the functions with an example image:** Calls the **display_results** function with an example skin lesion image to test the functionality.

This example demonstrates the complete process of building and deploying a health AI application for diagnosing skin diseases using deep learning and image processing techniques in Python using TensorFlow and OpenCV.

Appendices

Glossary Of Terms:

In the realm of artificial intelligence (AI) and Python programming, understanding the terminology and jargon is crucial for effective communication and comprehension. This glossary provides definitions for key terms and concepts commonly encountered in AI and Python-related discussions:

Artificial Intelligence (AI):

The simulation of human intelligence processes by machines, including learning, reasoning, problem-solving, perception, and language understanding.

Machine Learning (ML):

A subset of AI that enables computers to learn from data and improve their performance on specific tasks without being explicitly programmed.

Deep Learning:

A subfield of machine learning focused on neural networks with multiple layers (deep architectures), enabling the automatic learning of hierarchical representations from data.

Python:

A high-level, interpreted programming language known for its simplicity, readability, and versatility, widely used in AI, data science, web development, and scientific computing.

TensorFlow:

An open-source machine learning framework developed by Google for building and training deep learning models, known for its flexibility and scalability.

PyTorch:

An open-source deep learning framework developed by Facebook's AI Research lab, favored for its dynamic computation graph and ease of use in research and development.

1. **Natural Language Processing (NLP):** A branch of AI focused on enabling computers to understand, interpret, and generate human language, encompassing tasks such as text classification, sentiment analysis, and machine translation.

2. **Reinforcement Learning:** A type of machine learning where an agent learns to make decisions by interacting with an environment, receiving rewards or penalties based on its actions.

3. **Convolutional Neural Network (CNN):** A type of neural network designed for processing structured grid data, such as images, by using convolutional layers to extract features hierarchically.

4. **Recurrent Neural Network (RNN):** A type of neural network designed for processing sequential data, such as text or time series, by maintaining hidden state information across time steps.

5. **Transfer Learning:** A machine learning technique where knowledge gained from solving one problem is applied to a different but related problem, often by fine-tuning pre-trained models.

6. **Gradient Descent:** An optimization algorithm used to minimize the loss function of a machine learning model by iteratively adjusting model parameters in the direction of the steepest descent.

7. **Overfitting:** A common problem in machine learning where a model learns to fit the training data too closely, resulting in poor generalization to unseen data.

8. **Underfitting:** A common problem in machine learning where a model is too simple to capture the underlying structure of the data, resulting in poor performance on both training and test data.

9. **Hyperparameter:** A parameter of a machine learning algorithm that is set prior to training and influences the learning process, such as learning rate, batch size, or number of hidden units in a neural network.

This glossary serves as a reference for readers to clarify and deepen their understanding of key terms and concepts encountered throughout the book and in the broader field of AI and Python programming.

Python Syntax Reference:

Python is a powerful and versatile programming language widely used in various domains, including artificial intelligence, data science, web development, and system administration. This appendix serves as a reference for Python syntax, covering fundamental concepts and constructs essential for writing Python code effectively. Below are key syntax elements with explanations and examples:

1. **Variables and Data Types:**

Variable Declaration: Variables in Python are declared using the assignment operator (=). Python is dynamically typed, so variables do not require explicit declaration of data types.

```
x = 10
name = "John"
is_valid = True
```

Data Types: Python supports various data types, including integers, floats, strings, booleans, lists, tuples, dictionaries, and sets.

```
age = 25 # Integer
```

```
height = 5.11 # Float
name = "Alice" # String
is_valid = True # Boolean
```

Control Flow:

Conditional Statements: Conditional statements such as if, elif, and else are used to execute code based on certain conditions.

```
x = 10
if x > 0:
print("Positive")
elif x < 0:
print("Negative")
else:
print("Zero")
```

Loops: Python provides for loops and while loops for iterating over sequences and performing repetitive tasks.

```
for i in range(5):
print(i)
while condition:
print("Looping")
```

Functions and Modules:

Function Definition: Functions are defined using the def keyword, and can accept parameters and return values.

```
def greet(name):
return "Hello, " + name
result = greet("Alice")
```

Modules: Python modules are reusable code units that contain functions, classes, and variables. They can be imported into other Python scripts using the import statement.

```
import math
print(math.sqrt(16))
```

Lists, Tuples, Dictionaries, and Sets:

Lists: Lists are ordered collections of elements, which can be of different data types. They are mutable and indexed using integers.

my_list = [1, 2, 3, 4, 5]

Tuples: Tuples are immutable collections of elements, typically used to store heterogeneous data. They are indexed using integers.

my_tuple = (1, 'a', True)

Dictionaries: Dictionaries are unordered collections of key-value pairs, used for mapping keys to values.

my_dict = {'name': 'Alice', 'age': 25}

Sets: Sets are unordered collections of unique elements, used for mathematical operations like union, intersection, and difference.

my_set = {1, 2, 3, 4, 5}

Exception Handling:

Try-Except Blocks: Python provides try-except blocks for handling exceptions and errors gracefully.

try:

result = 10 / 0

except ZeroDivisionError:

print("Division by zero is not allowed")

This Python syntax reference provides a quick overview of essential concepts and constructs in Python programming. It serves as a handy reference for readers to consult while writing Python code for various projects and applications.

Additional resources:

In addition to the content covered in this book, there are numerous resources available for readers who wish to further explore topics related to artificial intelligence, Python programming, and related fields. This section provides a curated list of additional resources, including books, online courses, websites, and academic journals, to aid readers in their continued learning journey. Below are some recommended resources:

1. **Books:**

- *Python for Data Analysis* by Wes McKinney: A comprehensive guide to data manipulation and analysis in Python using tools like pandas, NumPy, and matplotlib.
- *Deep Learning* by Ian Goodfellow, Yoshua Bengio, and Aaron Courville: An authoritative textbook on deep learning techniques and algorithms.
- *Natural Language Processing with Python* by Steven Bird, Ewan Klein, and Edward Loper: A practical introduction to NLP techniques and applications using Python and the NLTK library.
- *Hands-On Machine Learning with Scikit-Learn, Keras, and TensorFlow* by Aurélien Géron: A hands-on guide to building machine learning models with popular Python libraries.

2. **Online Courses:**

- Coursera: Offers courses on a wide range of topics, including machine learning, deep learning, and Python programming, taught by leading instructors from universities and industry.
- Udacity: Provides nanodegree programs in AI, data science, and programming, with hands-on projects and personalized feedback.
- edX: Offers courses and certificates from top universities and institutions worldwide, covering AI, data science, and Python programming.

3. **Websites and Blogs:**

- Towards Data Science: A popular publication on Medium featuring articles and tutorials on data science, machine learning, and AI.
- Analytics Vidhya: An online community and platform for data science and machine learning enthusiasts, offering articles, tutorials, and competitions.

- ○ Stack Overflow: A question and answer website where developers can ask and answer programming-related queries, including those related to Python and AI.

4. **Academic Journals and Research Papers:**
   - ○ Journal of Machine Learning Research (JMLR): A peer-reviewed journal publishing articles on machine learning research and developments.
   - ○ Neural Computation: A journal covering research in computational neuroscience, neural modeling, and machine learning algorithms.
   - ○ arXiv: A preprint repository for research papers in various fields, including AI, machine learning, and natural language processing.

5. **Open-Source Projects and Repositories:**
   - ○ GitHub: A platform for hosting and sharing code repositories, where developers can find open-source projects, libraries, and frameworks related to AI and Python programming.
   - ○ TensorFlow Hub: A repository of pre-trained machine learning models and modules for TensorFlow, enabling easy integration into AI projects.

By exploring these additional resources and recommended readings, readers can deepen their understanding of AI, Python programming, and related topics, and stay updated on the latest developments and advancements in the field. Whether through books, online courses, websites, or academic journals, there are plenty of avenues for continued learning and exploration in the exciting and rapidly evolving field of artificial intelligence.